Engaging in Ministry with Older Adults

DOSIA CARLSON

An Alban Institute Publication

Library of Congress 1-56699-186-2
ISBN 1-56699-186-2

CONTENTS

92125

One of the ways I am truly blessed in my work as a senior consultant with The Alban Institute is the opportunity I have to engage material relevant to my own personal and spiritual path. Over the years I have found that I never really master a subject or a theory or a procedure until I am able either to teach it to others or to use it with others. My work with the issues of stress and burnout is a clear example. I was not prepared for the stress of being a senior consultant with the Institute nor was I able to deal with the burnout to which my workaholic tendencies inevitably led me, so I needed to learn for myself how to deal with these issues, in part by helping others with their own struggle. I had the same experience with spiritual formation: I needed to learn this for myself (my seminary training had in no way prepared me for the spiritual maturity that working at this level required), so I worked with others on their journeys.

As I began nearing the age of sixty, I recognized that I was avoiding the issue of my own aging process. I also recognized that I was not alone. Colleagues my own age or older were as busy as I was trying to deny the issues of aging, and most of the congregations with which I consulted desperately clung to the idea that unless younger people joined, the congregation was going to die. As a result they offered little of substance to older adults—for the most part patronizing their older members, rarely offering them anything of substance that dealt directly with their unique issues.

When I began to recognize my own, my colleagues', and congregations' avoidance of aging, I began to contemplate yet another learning I might incorporate into my work with the Institute. This was what motivated me to offer a seminar through Alban's educational department on the spirituality of aging. By trying to teach others about this subject, I hoped I would fully incorporate these learnings into my own life.

Having committed myself to that event a year in advance, I set about to learn as much about the subject as I could. One safeguard I gave myself was to team with a long-time friend, Emma Lou Benignus, age eighty-six, who has devoted the last fifteen years of her life to the subject of the spirituality of aging. Emma Lou had several things in print on the subject and had been called at the age of sixty-four to move to Valley Forge, Pennsylvania, to help American Baptist congregations to begin supporting in greater depth a ministry with older adults. She spent the next twelve years in that ministry.

One of Emma Lou's strengths and passions is her conviction that older adults have both the time and the skill to confront some of the more complex social issues of our times. When a retired older adult simply goes to the neighborhood school and sits in on a few classes to observe the quality of education being offered our young people today, that older adult can make an impact at the next school board meeting in that community.

Or a group of older adults who have a concern about how a local industry is affecting the environment can exercise that concern by each buying one share of stock in that company. Their status as shareholders gives them the right to attend the next stockholders or board of directors meeting, where they can assert themselves and ask board members some difficult questions about company policy. In this way, they can make an impact on society and our future life together in this nation. Many older adults feel this kind of freedom to speak out, a freedom they never seemed to have when they felt tied to the corporate world for their livelihoods. Emma and I came to call this "geezer power": older adults who have much less to lose speaking forthrightly for social justice and more compassionate social action on behalf of the poor or marginalized.

With the guarantee that Emma Lou would assist me with this work-shop, I then committed myself to attending a seven-day seminar with Rabbi Zalman Schachter-Shalomi, author of *From Age-ing to Sage-ing.* (As you will see, Dosia Carlson makes good use in this book of Zalman's insights and perspectives.) Zalman was well known as a spiritual guide before he engaged his own aging process and found himself forced to approach his life from a whole new perspective. Zalman makes the point in his books and seminars that we do not grow wise simply by growing older. Some people age with difficulty and bitterness, growing neither more compassionate nor wise, and other people come to terms with their aging and address some of the more frightening issues of their state, emerging from their struggles as joyful, grateful, wiser older people. These are people who have faced death squarely and are both unafraid and ready. Most importantly, they have done some heavy-duty life repair work, dealing with the givens of their life history, engaging in healing memories, and coming to a deeper understanding of how God was present with them through some of their most difficult life experiences. They are able to develop pearls of understanding from the pain that afflicted them in former times.

Finally, I felt ready to try teaching what I had been learning. The first workshop was held in Phoenix, Arizona, Dosia Carlson's backyard. Never having met her or known of her work, I was unaware of the resource on this subject that I had in that city. Emma Lou had known Dosia from other conferences on aging, however, and had told me about her. So it was a very pleasant surprise when, unannounced, Dosia showed up at the retreat center wanting simply to meet me and to understand more deeply what I was up to in this seminar. Thanks to Emma Lou, I was aware of the honor with which I was being blessed!

In the few hours we were able to spend together, I was impressed with her courage and determination. Having had polio as a teenager, Dosia gets around mainly in a wheelchair. She demonstrated to me how she is able to drive her station wagon by using a remote control pulley system that allows her to load and unload her wheelchair independently. When I saw this operation I understood one reason why she is so good at what she does: Her physical limitations have no doubt helped her develop an empathy for older adults who may also be limited physically. But her ministry embraces all older people, no matter how active or inactive they may be.

In our time together I found Dosia to be a most positive and inspirational human being. I was impressed with her background work on the subject of older adults. I soon realized that she was carrying out within the congregation where she works the kind of ministry we were trying to teach others about at this seminar.

You will like what Dosia offers you. Here are practical steps you can take to implement a quality ministry with older adults. Dosia also takes on the ageist culture in which we live and helps all of us see how we look at older adults in terms that diminish. And she holds out the possibility for rich intergenerational work that can go on within a congregation. In fact, congregations are one of the few institutions in our culture that have intergenerational potential built right into the fabric of their lives. Yet how little use we make of these opportunities!

You will also appreciate Dosia's challenge to older adults to grow in grace and faith. From what I have seen in most Christian congregations, we continue to offer them pap instead of the meaty stuff upon which they are eager to chew. Older adults need to be challenged with substantive material on the faith, and they have both the time and the inclination to wrestle with the deeper issues of life. Dosia will guide you in offering such challenges.

C'mon, let's grow older together. Let's do it in such a way that we learn and grow right until our very end. And let this be the best time of our lives as we also learn to savor the gift of merely being alive and conscious. By doing so, let's model for the millions of baby boomers who will soon reach retirement age how to grow older with joy and grace.

Dosia's book is one giant step forward in ministry with older adults. I am grateful for another opportunity to talk about something I really need to learn for myself, and for the opportunity to be a kind of John the Baptist for Dosia Carlson. I wish you well as you drink deeply of her insights and experience.

Roy M. Oswald

ACKNOWLEDGMENTS

How grateful I am to everyone who helped make this book a reality:

- Tuck and Bobbie Gilbert who initiated ideas about this project

- Individuals and congregations highlighted in each Engaging Example

- Dr. Steven Sterner and other supportive colleagues at Church of the Beatitudes

- Helen Pitts and volunteers at the Flinn Learning Center of the Beatitudes Center for Developing Older Adult Resources (Center D.O.A.R.)

- Jim Davis who kept me on friendly terms with my computer

- Nadine Smith and Esther Rings who critiqued the manuscript and always encouraged me

- All my aging friends who continue demonstrating how we can minister to one another as we grow older

- Greta Wiseman and her mother, Helen, who provided a quiet, nurturing environment while I buried myself at the computer. Without their aid I could not have finished this book. (And now I have no excuse for not helping in the kitchen!)

INTRODUCTION

When Alban Institute leaders envisioned a book about ministry with
older adults, they wanted to emphasize what congregations are doing
and could do in this critical area. Such a practical approach of letting
churches, synagogues, and individuals share their stories appealed to
me. It would give me an opportunity to incorporate insights from various
faith groups and diverse parts of the nation.

In a very real sense this resulting book is for congregations and by
congregations. Woven through each chapter are numerous references to
what is currently happening in such different settings as rural Iowa, a
Cleveland suburb, communities across the state of Oklahoma, a private
home in Massachusetts, and an ecumenical camp in the mountains of
Arizona.

I met many of my contacts for these stories during years of involvement in major organizations that combine emphases on both religion and
aging: the Forum on Religion, Spirituality and Aging of the American
Society on Aging; the National Interfaith Coalition on Aging now affiliated with the National Council on the Aging; the Federation of Interfaith Volunteer Caregivers; and the Shepherd's Centers of America. At
one point I served simultaneously on the governing bodies for each of
the first three groups. All that flying around the country and spending
long hours sitting at conference tables now has a new purpose—it provides connections among people doing distinctive older adult ministries.

In addition, I have found a fresh justification for being a pack rat.
During the last quarter of a century, I have been accumulating file fold-
ers filled with experiences related to the subject of this book. Several
file drawers bulge with details about Friendly Adults, a fellowship group
at Church of the Beatitudes created to help meet needs of older members

in this congregation. Since that group began some twenty years ago, I
have served as staff adviser. Other drawers hold the history of the
Beatitudes Center for Developing Older Adult Resources, Center
(D.O.A.R.), described in chapter 10. As founder and executive director
of that interfaith ministry, I worked with over one hundred congregations, listening to their stories about concerns and celebrations regarding older members.

My "storehouse of stuff" includes remnants from earlier years when
I was on the staff of the Beatitudes Campus of Care, a multilevel retirement facility. For over twenty-five years I have retained an association
with this home accommodating seven hundred residents. These aging
friends plus administrators and family members keep teaching me.

Additional insights reflected in this volume have arisen from my
participation in numerous seminars, retreats, conferences, and conversations. I am indebted to seminary students at Pacific School of Religion and Iliff School of Theology where I have taught courses about
helping churches develop and deepen ministries with older members
and their families.

Common issues emerging in various situations focused not only on
the how-to questions but also the sometimes deeper why-do questions.
This volume does not attempt to provide a step-by-step formula for
organizing senior members into clubs. Several good publications listed
in the bibliography address that concern. Moreover, I do not pretend
this book addresses every issue related to older adult ministries. Instead,
these chapters focus on ways that people in their later years can relate
faith and living. While acknowledging diminishing abilities that may
occur with longevity, I concentrate on positive examples of creative
lives and congregations in mission.

Engagement is a key word in this book. These pages tell of engaging faith communities in later life ministries. Every chapter includes
"Engaging Examples," authentic accounts of what has happened as
God's people seek meaning in their later years. Gerontology courses
several decades ago stressed two theories of aging: an activity theory
and a disengagement theory. Neither theory is complete. Indeed, older
people experiencing multiple losses may choose or be forced to reduce
involvements in society, but they need not disengage from spiritual
growth. A philosophy and theology of engagement challenges all of us
to nurture each other in lifelong abundant living, exercising God's gifts
for wholeness.

In these pages congregations will find information about the aging process as well as about implications for ministry. In addition to being beneficial for churches and synagogues, this book has a place in seminary education. Study groups may find especially useful the "Points to Ponder" page concluding each chapter. The questions found on those pages can also stimulate older readers to reflect on their life pilgrimage. If the illustrations sprinkled generously throughout the book motivate readers to adapt ideas or create their own responses to identified needs, then faithful engagement can result.

If you find this book engaging, go out to engage others in the enormous and fulfilling mission of developing creative ministries with older adults!

CHAPTER 1

The Graying
of Our Congregations

What Is Going On?

We cannot escape it—our nation has an increasingly aging population. Newspapers, television, Internet correspondence—all communication media remind us again and again that we have a longer life expectancy than our grandparents or parents did. We continually read and hear about the impact of shifting demographics on our national economy, our health care industry, and care-giving issues. But what about our churches and synagogues? How are we responding to the opportunities and challenges we find in the graying of our congregations?

When traveling across the United States, I am increasingly aware of the good news and the bad news about how faith communities are seeking to engage older members in ministry.

• In San Antonio, Texas, an Anglican church helped low-income older people obtain free grapefruit. The church's hospitality led to faith discussion groups, Bible study, and new members. Elderly women in the parish, assisted by these new members, started cooking food for homebound neighbors.

• Several congregations in New England rejected requests to provide space in their sanctuaries for wheelchairs. "Any alterations might mar architectural beauty."

• An interfaith group in Indiana meets regularly to review books about aging, such as *Affirmative Aging: A Creative Approach to Longer Life* edited by Joan Lukens.[1] Between meetings they seek ways to introduce workable ideas from the books into their community.

• A minister near Philadelphia reports what happened when she spoke about growing older to the XYZ (Extra Years of Zest) Club. One man in his sixties stood up and practically screamed, "Don't talk about aging! I don't ever want to hear that word."

• In New Mexico a retired priest-artist now in his eighties paints desert scenes. He sells his paintings to raise funds for an inner-city mission serving homeless men.

Each of the situations above gives a glimpse of what is going on in the aging arena. But how can we eradicate bad news and instead concentrate our energies on creating good news? To help answer that question we need to explore sources of ageism.

Beyond Ageism

Why are some people afraid of growing older? One reason may be their desire to remain as independent as possible for as long as possible, a theological dilemma further explored in chapter 6. As is true for so many fears, we become anxious about what we have not experienced. Because we must each experience our own aging, we may feel uncertain about making decisions regarding such matters as housing, financial concerns, and physical well-being.

My own experiences and study lead me to believe that much fear about aging comes from stereotypes. The greeting card industry is only one source of messages suggesting that to be old is to be useless. "Over the hill" party themes come in packages complete with black crepe paper. Television and other media often glorify youth. Even such a famous painting as Grant Wood's *American Gothic*, showing rigid husband, wife, and pitchfork, portrays an inflexible older couple.

When I have asked young people to make a list of words associated with the word *old*, they invariably give positive attributes to old objects such as cars, wine, and shoes. However, in the human arena their associations with *old* often include more derogatory connotations such as old geezer, dirty old man, old maid, and old biddy. Many of these youth were active in church fellowship groups. Are churches contributing to ageism by fostering fears and stereotypes?

Of course, myths flourish about any generation including teenagers and baby boomers. To help people examine attitudes toward age groups, try using the "Stages of our Ages" exercise. Depending on the size of the group filling out the chart, you may suggest that participants work individually, in pairs, or in triads. In every box in each column have participants write a single word that they associate with the designated age group. The column headings can be defined as follows:

- an adjective—word used to describe that age group
- an activity—what people at this age like to do
- an article—some toy or object prized by a specified age group
- an ally—category of person important at this age

Without identifying which age level is being described, have participants read their set of words. As others attempt to guess which age group the words describe, lively discussion may ensue. For example the words *sloppy*, *skateboard*, *boom box*, and *gangs* convey for some older people their image of teenagers. On the other hand, young adults may attach the following words to people over age eighty-five: *cranky*, *sleep*, *wheelchair*, and *nurse*. Both responses reveal prejudices that may indicate lack of intergenerational contact or understanding.

Forward through the Ages
One-worders on the Stages of Our Ages

	Adjective At this age people seem to be...	Activity At this age people like to...	Article At this age a precious thing is...	Ally At this age a significant person is...
1. Birth to age 1 year				
2. Age 1 to 6				
3. Age 7 - 12				
4. Age 13 - 18				
5. Age 19 - 29				
6. Age 30 - 39				
7. Age 40 - 64				
8. Age 65 - 74				
9. Age 75 - 84				
10. Age 85 +				

In 1994 the American Association of Retired Persons (AARP) conducted extensive research to determine what images Americans have about aging and older adults.[2] The project also explored how perceptions about aging and older people differ among children, teenagers, and adults. The results have significant implications for churches:

• Most Americans tend to exaggerate the health problems, loneliness, and financial difficulties of older people.

• Groups that have traditionally been deprived of economic and societal resources (African-Americans, Hispanics, women, and low-income groups) display the highest level of anxiety about aging.

• Children while still very young exhibit negative stereotypes of aging and older people.

• The 1994 results (similar to results of studies conducted in the 1970s and 1980s) tend to ascribe more problems to older people than were actually reported by those age sixty-five and older.

• Teens who have contact with older individuals at least a few times a month are more likely to report that the time spent with older individuals is enjoyable.

• Almost nine in ten of those age sixty-five or older say they are satisfied with their lives.

This AARP study suggests that many Americans still accept myths about aging and to some degree see late life as a time of loneliness, ill health, and decline. However, older people view themselves, individually, as capable, involved, healthy, and willing to participate in society. Older Americans have lifetimes of experience in solving problems at home, at work, in the community, and in congregations. If inaccurate perceptions keep us from tapping these resources, we need to correct those misconceptions.

Figuring from Facts

Congregations cannot ignore trends in population and implications for
ministry. Admittedly, religious institutions exist to worship God, to care
for God's creation with acts of justice. Churches and synagogues may
prefer to limit themselves to acts of piety, disregarding turmoil and
changes in the wider world. But demographics matter, both within congregations and beyond.

Descriptions and predictions based on 1994 data from the U.S.
Bureau of the Census are revealing:

• People sixty-five or older represent 12.7 percent of the total population. The number of older Americans has increased by 2.1 million or 7
percent since 1990, compared with an increase of 4 percent for the
under-sixty-five population.

• Since 1900, the percentage of Americans over age sixty-five has more
than tripled.

• A child born in 1993 could expect to live seventy-five and a half
years, about twenty-five years longer than a child born in 1900.

• About 2.1 million people celebrated their sixty-fifth birthday in 1994
(5,600 per day). In the same year, about 1.7 million people sixty-five or
older died, resulting in a net increase of 385,000 (1,050 per day).

• By 2030, there will be about 70 million older people, more than twice
the number in 1990.

• People sixty-five years and older are projected to represent 13 percent
of the population in the year 2000 but will represent 20 percent by 2030.

Statistics go on and on, but what do they mean for our local congregations? How do they translate into action for churches in the process
of transformation?

Nationally Speaking

If the mission of the church extends beyond church property, then church leaders can benefit from knowing what is going on in the world. Although most of this book deals with topics related specifically to local congregations, I think it is helpful to sketch briefly national developments and their implications for individual situations.

Public Programs

In 1965 the Older Americans Act went into effect. Although Congress has altered this act over the decades, the purpose remains the same: to fund programs to enhance life for people over age sixty. Monies appropriated from this source in 1994 supported nutrition programs (over 230 million meals provided in 1994), transportation (40 million rides), information and referral (12 million responses), care visits (1 million visits), and legal counseling (1 million sessions). Under the Administration on Aging each state organizes area agencies on aging, contracting with local service providers. Every congregation can benefit from knowing how to access its area agency on aging. Your telephone *Yellow Pages* may list useful resources under "Senior Services." Many other federal agencies exist to help develop services for older people. These include the Administration on Aging and the National Institutes of Health.

Private Organizations

Special interest groups related to aging are manifold. The appendix of this book lists addresses for a number of these. The following five have a direct bearing on religious institutions.

• National Interfaith Coalition on Aging (NICA)
Organized in 1972, NICA is a direct outgrowth of the 1971 White House Conference on Aging. In 1990 it affiliated with the National Council on the Aging. Sponsored by national agencies of Jewish, Catholic, Protestant, and Orthodox religious bodies, NICA includes in

its mission developing and distributing resources, representing spiritual concerns of older Americans in public and private forums throughout the United States, and serving the professional and personal needs of those who work with older adults in local congregations and religious agencies.

• Forum on Religion, Spirituality and Aging (FoRSA)
Under the umbrella of the American Society on Aging, this forum fosters inquiry into the search for a sense of meaning and value in life. It is a nondenominational, multidisciplinary membership network of professionals interested in the religious and spiritual support of older adults. In addition to holding conferences in conjunction with the annual meeting of the American Society on Aging, FoRSA distributes a quarterly newsletter, "Aging and Spirituality."

• National Federation of Interfaith Volunteer Caregivers
Where would congregations be without volunteers who perform particular tasks, such as shopping and transporting, for people with special needs? Recognizing the importance of having congregations work together in such volunteer efforts, the Robert Wood Johnson Foundation in 1983 awarded twenty-five grants to interfaith groups who would provide assistance and in-home services to older people. These projects were so successful that the foundation expanded the program by helping to fund hundreds of Faith in Action groups. For further information, see the Engaging Example in chapter 5.

• Shepherd's Centers of America
This nationally acclaimed movement began in Kansas City in 1972 under the inspiration of Dr. Elbert Cole. Making heavy use of volunteers and the leadership abilities of retired people, the Shepherd's Center concept embraces four components:

- life maintenance: response to survival needs such as financial assistance, emergency food, meals on wheels, and chore services
- life enrichment: focus on recreational and educational needs with trips, classes, and social events
- life reconstruction: guidance as people move through transitions such as illness and bereavement
- life transcendence: assistance in probing theological and spiritual concerns through both study and worship

One of the Engaging Examples at the end of this chapter spotlights a local Shepherd's Center in action.

• American Association of Retired Persons
Perhaps the best known of all organizations for older people is the AARP. Membership is open to anyone who is at least fifty years old. Over the years AARP has had an interreligious liaison office that offers helpful resources to faith communities. You will find references to some of these materials in subsequent chapters of this book.

Higher Education

Community colleges as well as public and private colleges and universities realize the importance of equipping students for positions related to gerontology. If you have any such institutions in your region, contact them for information about courses related to aging. Many schools offer special classes designed for older learners. Their libraries may also have helpful information.

Seminaries and other institutions for theological education are only beginning to take seriously the challenge of assisting congregations with their older adult ministries. According to Melvin Kimble's article in *Aging, Spirituality, and Religion: A Handbook*, "Course offerings in pastoral care and ministry with the aging in theological education curricula have been conspicuous by their absence."[3]

One recent approach to remedy this lack of theological preparation is the establishment of the Center for Aging, Religion, and Spirituality (CARS) at Luther Seminary in St. Paul, Minnesota. Through such programs as the Geriatric Pastoral Care Institute, the center not only provides academic offerings, but also encourages research of religious and spiritual components in late-life experiences. Both leaders and participants come from a variety of faith backgrounds.

Denominational Developments

For nearly twenty-five years I have been observing religious groups develop and carry out their older adult ministries. Their varying approaches reveal to some extent how intentional they are about recognizing the current age wave in our country. Practically all denominations report that their average age of membership is getting older. This graying of the congregations brings rich opportunities as well as challenges to those in national positions who seek to empower ministries on the local scene. During this quarter of a century, I noted reactions in national offices ranging from the disparaging question, "What will we do with all these older people?" to the uplifting observation, "What rich blessings we have in the lives and mature spirits of seasoned members." Such mixed reactions are also common in local settings.

What are denominational leaders in aging offering their congregations? The list that follows gives only a few glimpses of creative developments across the nation. These illustrations also contain seeds of ideas that can be transplanted in neighborhood soil.

• The Association of Lutheran Older Adults (ALOA)
Started in 1992 as a dream of the Wheat Ridge Ministries, ALOA's goals include:

- empowering older adults for service to the church and society
- engaging older adults in a caring community
- challenging older adults to share the heritage of their faith with
  generations that follow

An annual celebration promoted by ALOA is a "Bless the Years" Sunday. Three optional dates are suggested, one in May (Older Americans Month), another in July, and a third in October. Not only does ALOA provide sermon helps related to the lectionary for those proposed Sundays, but it can also supply suggested orders of worship, prayers and collects, press releases, and other materials to help planners. According to "Encore Times," the ALOA newsletter, nearly eight hundred churches responded during the first year "Bless the Years" Sunday was promoted.

The upbeat motto of ALOA, "Celebrate and Serve!" comes alive in the celebrations that honor pastors observing the fiftieth anniversary of their ordination. These jubilees recall all the lives touched by each pastor: baptisms, support to ill or dying people, visitations to the lonely, couples united in marriage, thousands receiving the Lord's Supper. What a way to celebrate God's gifts!

Organizers of ALOA attribute much of their success to the enthusiastic regional volunteer associates scattered across twenty-one states.
These men and women both promote existing ALOA programs and also
assist congregations that want to help establish new ministries. No doubt
these volunteer associates help to popularize the Share the Years program.
Recognizing the wide range of experiences that seasoned Christians
have had, Share the Years gathers people for discussion of contemporary
issues. A guidebook from ALOA provides all necessary content for the
discussions, including pertinent scripture perspective and pivotal discussion questions.

When developing the Share the Years design, Lutheran leaders
wisely recognized that there are many people age sixty and older who
enjoy getting together from time to time for the sheer joy of being with
peers, eating together, and socializing. Others, for a number of reasons,
may be less enthusiastic about such meetings. The intent of Share the
Years is to involve both groups.

• Episcopal Society for Ministry on Aging (ESMA)
"Aging is the only way to live!" That validation-of-life statement appears on a bumper sticker available through the Episcopal Society for
Ministry on Aging. Such a positive outlook echoes the thrust of a basic
study book prepared by ESMA: *Affirmative Aging: A Creative Approach to Longer Life*.[4] Both the original and revised editions of this
publication include chapters by major leaders in the field of religion
and aging. Authors emphasize the need to "run toward" aging rather
than "run from" it. By opposing negative stereotypes of growing older,
this volume suggests ways that churches can capitalize on elder wisdom.

Since its inauguration at the 1964 General Convention of the
Episcopal Church, ESMA has worked to serve the spiritual, psychologi-
cal, and physical needs of older people and to maximize the use of their
unique gifts and talents in continuing contributions to church and society.
Similar to the Lutheran organization, ESMA also has a network of contact people located throughout the United States. Annual conferences
for ESMA highlight themes such as "Cross Currents of Cultures and
Generations."

"Network News," the ESMA newsletter, includes some innovative
samples of activities throughout the nation. For example, the Diocese of
Florida has a retiree data bank that contains information about the skills

of over one hundred retired people who are willing to give of their time and talents to the church. Listed are computer whizzes, landscape artists, executives, secretaries, and many more. This approach again underscores the valuable abilities of retired people.

One novel resource that ESMA has created is Quest. Fashioned as a game sheet, this answer-question venture is described as "a journey through scripture increasing our awareness of the stages of relationship between human being(s) and God." Basically, the game invites players to explore life themes through designated biblical passages. Instructions encourage participants to reflect on questions such as "What does this passage/story tell us about aging?"

Engaging Examples

Presbyterian Older Adult Ministry Network (POAMN)

Although most denominations make some provision for ministries with older adults, I will focus on the model developed by the Presbyterian Church (U.S.A.). My contact with POAMN includes working with their national staff, providing leadership for several of their events, and using their materials. The comprehensive approach of the Presbyterian Church continues to impress me.

As early as 1973, delegates at General Assembly, the national governing body, approved policy statements concerning the rights and responsibilities of older people. Throughout the next twenty-five years they designated staff positions and modest funding to promote issues related to aging. POAMN began in 1982 when sixteen synods and a number of presbyteries designated individuals to promote the development of older adult ministry in the middle governing bodies of the Presbyterian Church (U.S.A.). By 1992 POAMN tackled the task of creating a ten-year plan guiding them into the new century.

But dates are important only as they mark significant accomplishments. Underlying all programming are clear statements communicating an understanding of theological and biblical bases for developing older adult ministries. Realistic data reflecting the ballooning older population permeate messages from leaders. By emphasizing the implications of demographics for churches, those messages constantly remind church members why they need to cultivate effective ministries with aging people. Perhaps such consciousness-raising efforts help explain why attendance in recent years has doubled at national gatherings on older adult ministries.

The Task Force on Older Adult Ministry prepared a statement adopted in 1992 by the 204th General Assembly. It has meaning for all faith communities.

> Life is a gift of God, and aging is a natural part of living, involving the whole lifespan from birth to death. Older adults are not a different category of people, but are simply those people who have traveled further along the journey. An understanding of aging must therefore be concerned with all of life rather than only with the later years. This understanding of aging affirms that older adults, as well as people of all ages, need to continue to learn, to work, to love, to be open to new ideas and challenges, to enjoy a wide variety of interpersonal relationships, and to engage in constructive activity, both giving and receiving during all of life, and especially in the later years of life.[5]

Priorities established at the national level are intended to have an impact on the local scene. Indeed, these are issues that affect every congregation:

- education and leader development
- focus on racial and ethnic people
- attention to health care and housing
- education and action concerning abuse of older adults
- emphasis on intergenerational experiences
- attention to spirituality and aging
- global and ecumenical concerns

Accompanying these priorities are clearly stated strategies designed not only for local congregations but also for presbytery and synod level. Also commendable is the intentional way in which aging issues are integrated with other areas of ministry.

Creative minds in the Presbyterian Church (U.S.A.) regularly

produce relevant, user-friendly materials. Agenda, the newsletter published quarterly, contains current information pertaining to trends in
society, models of existing programs, human interest stories, plus descriptions of new resources. There are two videos with study guides.
The first, "Aging Me . . . Aging You . . . The Journey of a Lifetime,"
realistically presents aging and suggests models for ministry with older
people. The second, "Aging Me . . . Aging You . . . Exploring the
Issues," invites discussion of five topics: ageism, death and dying, care
for the care giver, spirituality and aging, and justice issues.

Each year the Presbyterians designate a week in May as Older
Adult Week. A special planning packet includes not only suggestions
for worship services but also ways to engage volunteers appropriately,
ideas for encouraging evangelism with, by, and for older adults, and
information about new resources.

Contact: Miriam Dunson, Associate for Older Adult/Family Ministries
Congregational Ministries Division
Presbyterian Church (U.S.A.)
100 Witherspoon Street, Room 2008
Louisville, KY 40202-1396
(502) 569-5487

The Shepherd's Center of Richmond, Virginia

What Dr. Elbert Cole began in 1972 as an interfaith ministry in Kansas
City, Missouri, has now spread to more than one hundred locations in
the United States and Canada. This movement involves older people
helping each other in four areas mentioned above: life maintenance, life
enrichment, life reorganization, and life celebration.

These "life tasks" came alive in Richmond where during 1995
approximately 350 volunteers gave in excess of 14,000 hours to keep
their Shepherd's Center vibrant. Some of these volunteers provided
transportation, grocery shopping, help with medical insurance claims,
and other free services for people sixty years and over. Other volunteers
organized and taught in the Open University, a series of classes held at
three different churches. Courses cover an amazing array of topics such
as languages, current events, travel, science, recreation, philosophy, and
the arts. There is no need for seniors to be bored in Richmond!

Support for this particular Shepherd's Center comes not only from the twenty-two member congregations, but also from corporations and numerous individual contributions. Modest tuition fees help cover costs of the Open University. But the true value of these Centers defies any price tag. As this Center links needs and interests with energy and creativity, the satisfying results are priceless. This model reminds us that congregations working together can create ambitious programs that no single congregation could achieve alone.

Contact: Janyce H. Olson, Executive Director
The Shepherd's Center of Richmond
4900 Augusta Avenue #102
Richmond, Va. 23230
(804) 355-7282

Points to Ponder

1. Based on your own experiences, what evidence do you have to show that we live in a society with a rapidly growing aging population?

2. Some congregations have notable examples of ministries that engage older people. Describe any congregations like this about which you have heard.

3. Why do some people want to deny the fact of growing older? How would you respond to a person who says, "Don't talk to me about aging"?

4. What insights about aging might emerge from using the "Stages of Our Ages" exercise? Remember, even this idea of trying to describe age groups is in itself a form of stereotyping.

5. Each community has a variety of private and public agencies devoted to serving the aging. These may be related to a community council, United Way operation, or some other means of organizing community resources. Some of these may be listed in the telephone *Yellow Pages* under Senior Services. What services are available in your community? Which ones are most pertinent for congregations to use?

6. National or regional offices for churches and synagogues vary dramatically in the kind of help they can offer to older adult ministries of
local congregations. What kinds of resources are available to you?

7. Review portions of this chapter dealing with programs developed by
the Association of Lutheran Older Adults and the Episcopal Society for
Ministry on Aging. Which ideas are relevant for your situation?

8. Read carefully the philosophical statement adopted by the 204th
General Assembly (1992) of the Presbyterian Church (U.S.A.) on page
13. Which concepts in that statement may be most difficult to
communicate? Which ones may be most readily accepted?

CHAPTER 2

Connecting the Generations

Why We Need Intergenerational Programs

As long as we human beings continue to have babies we will continue to deal with the succession of generations. Our language, traditions, beliefs —all aspects of acculturation depend on other human beings who teach us to love or to hate. Children need the wisdom of older people, and older people need opportunities to interact with the freshness of younger generations. Yet, too often in our congregations we segregate by age, encouraging each generation to see itself as separate rather than as an integral part of a larger community.

The University of Pittsburgh Generations Together program, in cooperation with other institutions, has prepared a publication outlining the importance of intergenerational provisions, reminding us that they help to:

- dispel stereotypes about young and old
- allow the strengths of one generation to meet the needs of another
- bring people together to address the needs of all ages through co-operation and pooled resources
- develop an appreciation for rich cultural heritage, traditions, and histories[1]

This booklet emphasizes the differences between today's mobile society and the traditional extended family of an earlier era. Grandparents, parents, and children may no longer be living together and sharing the responsibility of rearing children. Elders may not have the opportunity to enjoy the benefits of enthusiasm and learning from involvement in other generations. Many activities that traditionally took place in the home—caring for frail elders, minding young children, and teachings values and skills—are often neglected or done outside the family. This poses a challenge to churches and synagogues, encouraging us to develop innovative ways to help young and old interact in meaningful ways.

Generations in Opposition

"The battle of generations." What a disturbing phrase that is, yet we hear it in varying contexts. As we enter the twenty-first century, we are taking with us labels for people who were born in particular years. References abound to that group known as baby boomers. In 1996 the first-born baby boomers turned fifty years old. This group, born between 1946 and 1964, represents the largest generation ever in the United States. Their presence will affect all arenas including public policy as well as church programming.

Following behind the baby boomers is Generation X, which includes "slackers"–young adults who are often characterized as under-employed. Many in this generation prefer to delay the birth of children. Many who are in this group, born between 1968 and 1978, resist being labeled. Some social scientists suggest that this group has lost a sense of community.

And then we have "the children." Appalling statistics haunt us regarding conditions of the youngest members of our human race. In the United States a child is reported abused or neglected every ten seconds; every thirty-two seconds a baby is born into poverty; every fifteen minutes a baby dies. These outrageous conditions spurred on those who organized the 1996 Stand for Children Day in Washington, D.C. Who will serve as advocates for the most vulnerable section of our population?

What about "the old folks"? To champions of younger ages, those people living into their eighties, nineties, and one hundreds pose a threat. Shapers of public policy may agonize over allocations of resources. Too many people are quick to point fingers at Social Security or Medicare as the culprits responsible for budget deficits. The derogatory term *greedy geezer*, applied to people who are perceived as self-serving, reflects hostility fueling flames of intergenerational conflict.

Such conflicts, whether real or imagined, result in lively debate. To help focus this debate, the AARP in 1993 published *Justice Across Generations*.[2] Rabbi Harlan Wechsler, author of the opening chapter, noted three Talmudic obligations relating generation to generation: the obligation of parents toward children, the obligation of young people toward all old people, and the obligation of children to elderly parents. In addition to citing the commandment to honor mother and father, he stressed the need for mercy and compassion as well as for justice.[3]

Has the conflict between generations been exaggerated? Some researchers insist that although the perception of generational inequity is widespread, in reality generations are pulled together by "hidden connections" characteristic of democratic beliefs in equality. Contrary to the bumper sticker quip "I'm spending my children's inheritance," the private transfer of goods and services thrives. Moreover, families rooted in a faith community have an additional bond.

As a delegate to the 1995 White House Conference on Aging, I sensed a genuine effort to recognize the need for cooperation among the generations. In contrast to the three previous White House conferences, official youth delegates participated. Although the resolutions attracting the most votes centered on economic security, there was a resolution specifically addressing the need to advocate for children. A portion of that resolution urges that we "engage the productive and humanitarian potential of the older population to meet the human, educational, social, environmental, health, and cultural needs of children." That is a huge, vital agenda!

Do our churches contribute to generationalism? In your own situation, do budgetary and programming considerations in your congregation pit one generation against another? What responsibilities do adults have for communicating the good news to younger minds and hearts? Recalling the adage "Christianity is only one generation from extinction," I would add that sustaining our faith depends on telling our story from generation to generation. This chapter will focus on ways to keep that story alive.

Common Examples of Connecting Generations

Your congregation may already provide many opportunities for young and old to interact. Even if you are located in a retirement community, you may be cultivating ties with children or youth.

The Sacrament of Holy Baptism incorporates a person into the universal church, the body of Christ. When an infant or young child is baptized, the parents and sponsors promise to assume special responsibilities for the Christian nurture of the one baptized. Moreover, the entire congregation promises to help in that nurturing. Women in St. John United Church of Christ, Defiance, Ohio, celebrate each baptism by creating a personalized blanket plus a stole for the person receiving baptism. Started by older members of the Women's Guild, this significant tradition continues as women of all ages crochet, knit, or quilt blankets. They artistically cross-stitch each stole with the baptized's name, date of baptism, and appropriate symbols including the church logo. Those receiving such stoles and blankets tell in later years of how significant that gift becomes.

Worshipping together is another example of connecting generations. Yet, this can cause controversy. Informal surveys in several churches reveal that many parents desire "quiet time" during worship. They report that trying to control youngsters distracts them from centering on the service. One response to that concern is to provide within the space used for worship a special corner or other area where children can engage in quiet activities. Some congregations invite children of designated ages to be with families during the opening portions of worship. Following a customized "word with the children," these young people then depart for their own educational program. Older members often comment that they look forward to seeing the young ones with their parents. For some, this may be the only time during a week when they even see young life. Greeters near the sanctuary front door can include various generations. In fact, when children as well as parents or grandparents shake hands, this reminds everyone, including visitors, that all ages are welcome.

Holidays become natural times for creative interaction. Christmas workshops offer many such opportunities. With skillful planning, usually requiring months of preparation, participants from ages two to ninety-two and beyond can enjoy activities such as making wreaths, baking and decorating cookies to share with homebound individuals, or making

Christmas tree ornaments. Before or after a Christmas caroling outing is a great time for a party designed to help young and old know each other better and to probe the deeper meaning of the season.

Other holidays also provide opportunities for intergenerational contacts. Around Halloween a couples club in an Oregon church arranges transportation to bring homebound members to their fellowship hall. Club members, in addition to bringing their own families, also ask other families with children to join in the festivity. Pumpkin carving and decorating consumes much energy. Other fellowship-building activities and games help all ages become better acquainted. Easter, Thanksgiving, Fourth of July, the start of a new calendar year or school year—any special date suggests possibilities for older and younger sharing faith, fun, and food.

Shared meals really can be sacramental. Rather than advertising "another potluck," develop themes that bring generations together. The creative arts are a good starting place. Although music at times drives generations apart, churches can encourage teenagers, parents, and grandparents to spend time—perhaps over a meal—listening constructively to each other's music. Dramatic productions need not be huge Broadway spectaculars, but enlightening or entertaining one another through published and original plays involves multiple skills. Adolescents may choose to help with stage construction, props, or costumes. What a good opportunity for them to learn with help from older people. Sensitive leadership may recognize teachable moments when generations authentically share basic values, frustrations, and joys.

Additional Ways to Connect with Children

When designing special activities for your church to connect older people with children through elementary school age, keep several guidelines in mind:

• Designate clearly who is responsible for organizing, executing, and evaluating; preferably this will be done by a volunteer committee.

• Explain to each group the reasons for connecting; these might include such reasons as fellowship, completing a service project, or sharing special skills or stories with each other.

• When possible, have an initial meeting with small groups interacting; large gatherings tend to lead to confusion.

• If you are starting a prolonged project such as establishing pen pals or phone pals, keep the project time-limited; if the response is very enthusiastic, the project can always be extended.

• Give participants time to share their reactions, both positive and negative.

Selected activities will vary depending on the ages and level of functioning of those involved as well as such factors as time available, leadership resources, and funding. The following list is simply suggestive; be creative and experiment with your own ideas.

• Prepare holiday favors to take to homebound people or residents in nursing homes. Of course, there is no need to limit such activity to holiday time. Look for other events to celebrate: birthdays, anniversaries, special events in community or nation, changing seasons.

• Create a collage from magazine pictures. These could be "all about me" self portraits that could be displayed in some area of the church. This would also help others outside the intergenerational group become more aware of church people.

• Organize reading sessions with younger people reading to older when appropriate or older reading to younger. You can find excellent books written for the primary purpose of helping young and old understand each other better. Perhaps an intergenerational group can raise funds to purchase church library books such as the following:

Ackerman, Karen. *By the Dawn's Early Light*. New York: Macmillan, 1994.
A grandmother feeds dinner to her two grandchildren, helps them with their homework, and puts them to bed while their mom works the graveyard shift at a factory in this touching, realistic child's view of a difficult situation.

Dugan, Barbara. *Loop the Loop*. New York: Greenwillow Books, 1992.

A friendship develops between a little girl and her eccentric wheelchair-bound, yo-yo-slinging elderly neighbor and endures when the neighbor breaks her hip and must move to a nursing home.

Fox, Mem and Julie Vivas. *Wilfrid Gordon McDonald Partridge.* Brooklyn, N.Y.: Kane Miller, 1989.
A small boy tries to discover the meaning of memory so he can restore that of an elderly friend.

Polacco, Patricia. *Mrs. Katz and Tush.* New York: Dell, 1992.
A runty, tailless kitten brings together an African-American boy and his widowed Jewish neighbor. This pair enrich each other's lives with their similarities and differences.

Sakai, Kimiko. *Sachiko Means Happiness.* San Francisco: Children's Book Press, 1990.
A Japanese-American girl hates spending time alone with her grandmother, who has Alzheimer's disease, until she realizes just how frightening it must be to be surrounded by people you do not recognize.

Bringing Youth and Age Together

Junior high and high school students usually exude energy and imagination. At times their own struggles of moving through adolescence can seem to devour them. How can they interact with older people in ways that will be mutually beneficial?

Many denominations establish the teenage years as the time for confirmation preparation. Theological thinking is not beyond the ability of young people. One way to assist them in probing their faith is to provide mentors, mature men and women who are willing to walk beside students as they contemplate confirmation. Older people can be outstanding mentors. Those willing to do more listening than talking may serve most effectively in the mentoring role.

The Center on Rural Elderly published a remarkable *Directory of Intergenerational Programming.*[4] It contains 173 descriptions of programs designed to bring young and old together. Ideas could easily be adapted for rural or urban settings, for community centers, for schools, or for religious institutions. As I read through this directory, I noticed intriguing acronyms. Even these titles suggest directions for developing programs:

HOSTS—Hands of Shared Time
ETC—Elderly-Teen Connection
TLC—Teaching-Learning Communities
SEASONS—Senior Experts and Speakers on Numerous Subjects
ECHO—Elders and Children Helping Each Other
FLIP—Friendly Listener Intergenerational Program

Many of the references in this directory describe service projects with youth doing tasks for or with elders. So long as the relationship does not become patronizing on the part of either generation, the element of direct service can precipitate healthy interaction.

Even as today's seniors cannot be lumped into one mold presuming they are all alike, so too those who range in age from thirteen to early twenties are astoundingly different from one another. Not all of them belong to gangs, deal in drugs, have children out of wedlock, or drop out of high school. Such behaviors are symptoms of our fractured society and are issues that churches must address. But there are other faces of youth desperately longing to make some sense out of apparent chaos. They may feel righteously indignant about violations of our environment or tolerating racism.

Metropolitan Baptist Church, Pensacola, Florida, has a successful Extended Arms program for youthful offenders. A judge may sentence them to this program. Three times a week, juvenile first and second offenders gather at the church for counseling on alcohol, drugs, and anger; for emotional or family counseling; and for tutoring in a program coordinated with their teachers. And who helps to keep this program alive? Volunteers include those who could well be the grandparents of the offenders.

Because teenagers often feel more comfortable when supported by their peers, they may respond to ideas about work parties. What congregation does not have older people who need help to maintain their homes? Where are the young people who, with proper motivation, could cut grass, trim shrubbery, wash windows, paint inside and outside houses? Congregations need to be aware of who needs what kind of help and who might be able to meet those needs. Work parties involving groups of youth could be part of the solution. In some cases, older widows, grateful for the attention and services of the young people, have reciprocated by providing treats such as hot chocolate and home-baked cookies. Now that is really connecting the generations!

Supporting Adult Children with Aging Relatives

Large numbers of adult children find themselves needing to care for those who once mothered and fathered them. Problems may develop in areas such as transportation, choice of housing, physical changes, depression, and legal matters. Too often both generations need someone who will listen to them. Frequently as I travel around the country, often by air, I have casual conversations with strangers. When they learn of my background in gerontology, they often respond with, "Let me tell you about my parents."

A relatively new term describing an increasingly common concern is *sandwich generation*. This refers to people, usually in mid-life, who are caring for both younger and older generations. A working mother may have responsibilities for her school-age children as well as aging parents or grandparents. Because relationships may become rather sticky, some folks in jest suggest we use the term *peanut butter sandwich generation*.

Any family member or friend sharing responsibility for an older person may experience reactions such as frustration, guilt, and exhaustion. They often find themselves asking questions like "Why can't anyone give me a straight answer? How do I know if I am doing too much or too little? Won't I ever have any time for myself?"

Relationships between adult children and their parents, grandparents, or other relatives need not be negative. Congregations can offer help and hope for such situations. Church libraries are a starting point for locating resources. Books about caring for older parents are pouring off the presses. The very titles suggest issues related to this population:[5]

When Love Gets Tough: The Nursing Home Decision
Taking Time for Me
Parentcare Survival Guide
When Living Alone Means Living at Risk: A Guide for Caregivers and Families

Congregations can sponsor support groups initiated by a committee, a governing board, or individuals with special interest in this area. Such a group might result from a four- to six-week study session based on helpful materials such as those just listed. Although it is advisable to have a facilitator with skills to help participants interact, often little more is needed than an invitation to share situations. In one setting a woman whose father had recently stopped driving helped another woman explore ways to resolve this problem and find alternatives for transportation. Insights gained from each other make support groups beneficial.

Although each family constellation has particular challenges, information available through church staff, newsletters, bulletin board announcements, and other forms of communication can address topics such as the following:

• hiring help for in-home care
• accessing community resources
• guiding long-distance care givers
• selecting a long-term care facility
• preventing depression for all generations

Sometimes care givers feel so overwhelmed with tasks that they fail to function well. Using a simple "Responsibility Tree" may help clarify and prioritize what needs to be done. In the appropriate circle, write the name of each person for whom you feel responsible. You might rank the names (A, B, and C, for example) to indicate how much responsibility you carry. Use the spaces at the bottom to note the responsibilities you have for the relationships you marked as needing the most of your responsibility.[6]

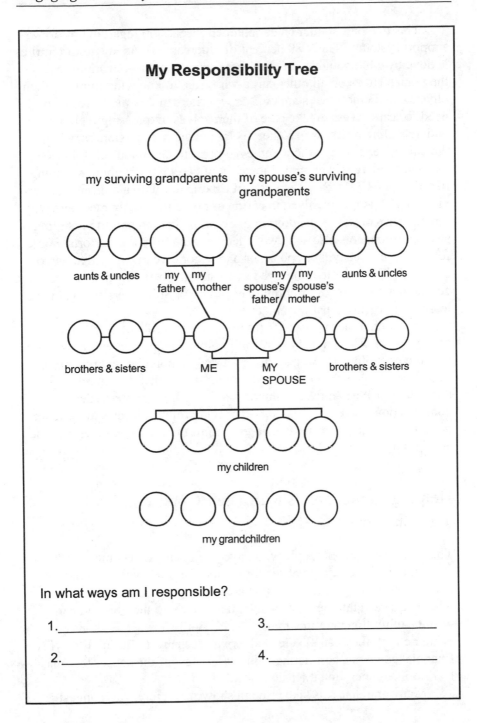

My Responsibility Tree

my surviving grandparents   my spouse's surviving grandparents

aunts & uncles   my father / my mother   my spouse's father / my spouse's mother   aunts & uncles

brothers & sisters   ME   MY SPOUSE   brothers & sisters

my children

my grandchildren

In what ways am I responsible?

1._____   3._____

2._____   4._____

    This tree or a similar chart can open discussion regarding informal
support systems. Nearly 80 percent of eldercare provided within families
is done by adult daughters. Often these women are also working outside
the home. They and all other caregivers need to know the limits of their
physical and emotional stamina. Many writers in this field stress the
need for care givers to take care of themselves. Expressing feelings to
understanding peers, as in a church class or support session, may help
the care giver avoid burnout and even prevent elder abuse.

    Do we dare talk about the rewards of caregiving without sounding
like Pollyanna? Research analysts in Champaign-Urbana, Illinois, interviewed 412 people involved in caring at home for family members with
Alzheimer's disease.[7] In addition to being realistic regarding resulting
stress, respondents also acknowledged benefits from their efforts. Some
felt they were repaying a spouse or parent for care given by that person
earlier. Others reported improved self-esteem when they discovered they
could do a good job of providing needed help. Still others saw value in
learning to be more patient and tolerant.

    In our churches we can affirm the important role of care givers in
several ways. We can identify respite volunteers, people willing to come
into the home to give the care giver a break. Appreciation brunches or
even brief retreats for care givers let them know that the church cares
about their needs. At the minimum, staff and appropriate leaders of
congregations have an obligation to provide referral information. If we
do not have an answer, we can at least point the way to sources of hope
and help.

Helping Grandparents with Their Opportunities
and Challenges

The majority of older people who have been parents become grandparents and often are also great-grandparents. Families with four and five
generations living at the same time are no longer a surprise to us. In
what ways can churches and synagogues enter into the joys and frustrations of multigenerational family life? While new generations can
bring delight, they can also lead elders to despair. Differing lifestyles,
financial concerns, conflicting values are a few of the causes that may
lead to intergenerational tensions.

    Many grandparents take pride in showing pictures of youngest branches on the family tree. Why not establish a church bulletin board to display periodically pictures of different members within one family unit. This "Meet the Family" board could serve another useful purpose of enabling the rest of the congregation to become more aware of who is related to whom.

Although grandparenting has usually been considered a "learn on the job" role, this task has become increasingly complex. Robert and Shirley Strom of Scottsdale, Arizona write and teach extensively about this very topic. Their primary publications are *Becoming a Better Grandparent* and *Achieving Grandparent Potential*.[8] Each publication consists of two volumes: The first contains articles known as viewpoints, the second is a guidebook with useful worksheets intended for use by all generations. The authors present guidelines with questions for engaging young and old in discussing topics such as friends, travel, boredom, sports, war, and religion. Their materials can easily be adapted for use by congregations.

By presenting their philosophy about how generations interact, the Stroms remind us that at the turn of this century, and for centuries before, people gave significant attention to honoring the past. That emphasis contributed to an attitude of respect for aging people. Moving into the twenty-first century, people now focus more on the future. Will we have nuclear war? Do we have sufficient food, water, and fuel for life on planet earth? Answers from the past may seem irrelevant. Thus, grandparents who say "When I was your age . . ." have not experienced what children or teenagers experience living in the electronic, "information" age. Yet, today's grandparents often communicate by e-mail; and what they share may reflect wisdom and values garnered from decades of living. Finding ways to help grandparents, their children, and their children's children grow in faith will continue to be a challenge to churches and synagogues.

What about those grandparents who have the full-time responsibility for parenting their grandchildren? This is becoming a more common situation. In fact, researchers estimate that about one out of every twenty children is being raised by a grandparent with no parent living in the home. The most common reasons for this situation to develop are that one or both of the parents may be addicted to drugs, may be alcoholic, a teenager, seriously ill, violent, missing, or deceased.

Support groups for these grandparents are mushrooming all over the country. If there are not enough people in one congregation to warrant a gathering, consider sponsoring such a group jointly with other congregations in your community. Issues to address on behalf of grandparents and their grandchildren include investigation of child abuse, neglect, or abandonment; need for financial help; guidance from the legal system; and involvement with school and other agencies.

Recognizing the critical problems in so many of these households, the AARP has established the Grandparent Information Center. The Center can provide helpful booklets and guidance for those wanting to start local support groups for grandparents raising grandchildren. To reach their Washington, D.C. office, call (202) 434-2296.

Developing Extended Families

For seven years I have had the privilege of belonging to an intergenerational extended family organized through our congregation. Although we are all members of the same church, prior to joining this family we had little awareness of each other's inner joys and pains. Responding to an invitation from the Adult Education Committee, we began in a somewhat formal fashion. Within a few months we flowered into a close community of children, youth, men, and women who care deeply about each other. Our particular group of twenty-four people includes two families with elementary-age children, a family with youth—two of them now off to college, women who have never been married, several widows, a widower, one couple married several years ago—the bride in her seventies and the groom in his eighties, another retired couple whose grandchildren live out of the state.

Although our ages range from eight to eighty-four, the number of years we have lived is not important. What counts is caring. One year a teenager in our family, Corbin, suffered life-threatening wounds when another Boy Scout accidentally shot him. Our family immediately moved into action by bringing meals for relatives who were keeping an unbroken vigil in the intensive care waiting room. Equally important was surrounding Corbin and his family with emotional and spiritual support. We held prayer sessions in the hospital, church, and private homes across the city. Because our extended family roots were already deeply intertwined, we were able to meet this crisis with a level of caring I have seldom experienced.

In the 1970s, religious educators promoted the concept of family clusters. Margaret Sawin, acknowledged leader for this movement, developed extensive resources for helping churches offer family meetings as part of weekly church education. Her book *Family Enrichment with Family Clusters* gives detailed instructions for putting ideas into action.[9] Our much less structured extended family has only a few guidelines:

- We meet monthly, usually for a meal in one of the homes.
- We plan our own activities, seeking to include everyone in the activity.
- We select an outreach project in which we can become personally involved.
- We share, as appropriate, in celebrating special events in the lives of members.

We have attended recitals of children, gone together to parades and sports events, held a reception for one of our couples renewing their marriage vows, and caroled to homebound members. Each extended family can decide what is relevant. In our case, the outreach project involves financial support and monthly grocery shopping for a near-poverty level, inner-city family. Without our presence, the teenage sons might have dropped out of high school. Now they are contemplating junior college.

Extended families bring generations together in a natural, meaningful way. Having one or two people coordinate plans gives a minimal but useful sense of organization. As we break bread together, lift each other up in prayer, confess our needs and celebrate milestones, we catch a glimpse of what early Christians may have experienced.

Engaging Examples

The Committee on Program Enrichment for Seniors (C.O.P.E.S.)

The First Presbyterian Church of Fort Collins, Colorado, recognizes the importance of developing creative programs with its senior members and their families. With Marcia Richards working twenty-five hours a week as Director of Senior Adult Ministries, this congregation offers a rich variety of opportunities for service and growth. Those most involved in determining the direction of the ministry serve on the planning board known as C.O.P.E.S.

Particularly pertinent for this chapter is the way C.O.P.E.S. facilitates interaction among the generations. A yearly calendar of activities features the following:

- A college group decorates and delivers Christmas trees to some of the older adults.
- Junior high students make and deliver valentines to older members.
- Church school classes visit nursing homes.
- Young and old attend baseball games together.
- Elderly and youth pair together as prayer partners.

One activity I find especially appealing is the annual Grandparent/ Grandchild Day Camp. A typical schedule includes making creative name tags; time for singing; craft choices, including decorating baseball caps or tote bags; a field trip to a local attraction such as the Sweatsville Zoo; learning centers with guidelines for sharing faith issues, watching and learning dance steps, and a closing circle.

This is designed for children ages five to ten and their grandparents. If youngsters in that category have no readily available grandparents, however, they may be adopted by church members of grandparent age. Also, if those in the grandparent generation have no related child in the vicinity, they may adopt one of the children needing a relative.

Says staff person Marcia Richards, "I think it very unusual for a grandparent to spend six hours with a grandchild without a TV, computer, video, or video games! Everyone seems to have a great time. We even had participants decorate postcards, write messages, address them to the other generation, and mail them. We thought it might encourage the children to write letters."

In addition to fostering intergenerational experiences, C.O.P.E.S. sponsors seasonal celebrations, weekly Fitness, Fellowship, Faith gatherings, monthly potluck luncheons with stimulating programs, day trips, homebound visitation, Senior Adult Breakfast Club, Out-to-Lunch Bunch, educational forums, and Seniors of Service (S.O.S.). A descriptive brochure outlining this Senior Adult Ministry Program even has a paragraph entitled "Other Opportunities." All the examples can easily be adapted.

Contact: Marcia Richards, Director of Senior Adult Ministries
First Presbyterian Church
531 South College Avenue
Fort Collins, CO 80524
(970) 482-6107

Elderlife Ministry

The Federated Church, United Church of Christ, in Chagrin Falls, Ohio, boasts a thriving ministry involving approximately 450 older people from church and community. Started in 1983, Elderlife Ministry offers a variety of programs under the direction of Janet Peters, a twelve-member committee, and nearly 150 volunteers. Participants may choose from an inviting menu of activities that includes:

- Senior Adult Education Program incorporating courses taught by faculty from the local Cuyahoga Community College
- service project with the American Cancer Society
- field trips to nearby Cleveland and surrounding areas
- People Talk meeting twice weekly with speakers, Bible study, crafts, music, exercise, socialization, snacks
- men's group gathering twice a month for fellowship
- Elderlife monthly luncheon featuring diversified programs
- Sandwiched Generation, a support group for middle-generation people who have children and aging relatives, meeting twice monthly with a trained facilitator

An additional program in this congregation of 1,300 members bears the arresting name of "Oaks and Acorns." Once a month children gather at the church after school for a social time involving their parents and grandparents or grandparent substitutes. During the course of a year they play volleyball or other sports, challenge one another to board games, make favors for hospital patients, read books aloud, experiment with clown ministry, and go on picnic outings.

One grateful mother wrote, "I look forward to Oaks and Acorns days, and my kids do, too. It's fun and interesting to be with people whose experience extends to a time before my children and I were born. It's easy to live only in a world of the young family: school activities, business dinners, play groups, friends our own age. But it always feels like something is missing. I like a mixture. I like to know what it's like to be eighty years old, how it feels and what one thinks about and believes. I want my children to know that, too."

Contact: Janet Peters, Elderlife Ministry Director
Federated Church
76 Bell Street
Chagrin Falls, Ohio 44022
(216) 247-649

Points to Ponder

1. In your community, what agencies already exist for bringing generations together effectively?

2. In what ways, consciously or unconsciously, may your congregation be fostering intergenerational rivalry?

3. Which person or group(s) in your church does or could organize intentional intergenerational experiences?

4. The baptism of every infant and child offers your church an opportunity to bring old and young together. Consider significant symbolic acts you could introduce to celebrate baptism.

5. How do you show your community that your congregation believes in intergenerational ministries?

6. Check your church library to see what books and other resources you have to help adult children with aging relatives.

7. If your community has no support groups for adult children caring for

older people, consider starting one, perhaps in cooperation with another congregation or human service agency.

8. How might your church support care givers, including grandparents serving as parents?

9. If you believe extended families have a place in your congregation, how might you proceed to make them a reality?

CHAPTER 3

Nurturing Lifelong Learning

Learning as a Lifetime Process

From the moment of birth—and perhaps even earlier—our minds begin interacting with our environment. The phenomenon of how brains function, processing input from all the senses, is a source of wonder and praise.

Men and women in later years who have been accumulating knowledge for decades can continue learning throughout their life span. In a society in which computers and the media bombard us with new information, older learners are surrounded with opportunities to explore the world of ideas.

Congregations need to recognize the importance of keeping members alive to learning. Hebrew Scriptures and the New Testament remind us that we are "people of the Book." Both formal and informal educational processes are implied in the Bible. References to knowing commandments and teaching children the laws and traditions abound in the Pentateuch. Jesus sought to learn from the elders in the temple; as a rabbi, he was certainly a product of a religious education program. Repeatedly the gospels state that "he taught them as one who had authority" (Matthew 7:29).

School districts invest heavily in education for children, youth, and adults. Pedagogy explores ways to instruct young learners. School systems are broadening their curricula and offering classes for parents or adults of any age. Institutions across the nation are targeting older people as prospective students.

No faith community can long exist without providing stimulating sessions not only for youngsters but also for those who may be in the age range of grandparents or great-grandparents. With the graying of our congregations, we need to be particularly focused on designing learning opportunities that reflect interests and needs of the oldest generation. In addition to focusing on topics with biblical and theological emphases, classes can address current social or political issues. As will be noted later in this chapter, congregations do well to offer a wide variety of classes or small-group discussion gatherings. Yet, each subject should be understood to relate to the learners' heritage of faith.

What provisions do our congregations make for adult education? In particular, how intentional are we about providing opportunities for retirees or others in mature years to keep growing intellectually? Where can churches and synagogues find resources for developing stimulating courses? These and other questions will be discussed in this chapter.

The Older Learner

Recognizing that the adjective *older* is relative term, we can give rather generalized insights into the learning patterns of those who may be in their sixties, seventies, eighties, or beyond. Even as children learn in varying ways and exhibit diverse aptitudes for processing information, so too there is a wide range of learning abilities among older people. In fact, the oldest members of our society are often described as the most heterogeneous population in our nation. Although they may have experienced the same historical events, such as World War II and the emergence of the computer age, their reactions are by no means similar.

One element that can alter the processing of information is the changes in sensory perceptions that can come with aging. Changes in eyesight may be a significant deterrent to reading. Diminished hearing may also affect learning in a group setting. Reaction time becomes slower with age. That does not mean, however, that older people are incapable of learning new ideas; they may just need more time. This is especially true when they are trying to recall recently acquired information.

Geriatric physician Mark E. Williams writes encouraging words in his *Complete Guide to Aging and Health*: "The capacity to learn and adjust continues throughout life, strongly influenced by interests, activity, motivation, health, and income. With years of rich experience and reflection, some of us can transcend our own circumstances. We call this wisdom. Old age can be a time of variety, creativity, and fulfillments."[1]

Developing Learning Opportunities

Learning at Home

As congregations develop creative approaches to nurturing people in later years, they need to include in their planning the special needs of those who cannot easily attend church or synagogue activities. In this context, "home" refers not only to one's private dwelling place but also to congregate settings such as retirement facilities or nursing homes.

One of the Engaging Examples at the close of this chapter describes a course of study prepared for people in care facilities.

Men and women essentially homebound still have access to numerous sources of new information. Because many elderly may have VCR equipment, congregations can arrange to take selected videotapes to these more isolated members. Instead of just sending or delivering such resources, consider having volunteers spend time with the homebound person sharing video or audiotapes, discussing ideas, and stimulating each other's thinking.

With increased access to learning materials, such as books, newspapers, television, and computers, the number of solitary learners may increase. Even as home schooling is gaining in popularity among families of diverse backgrounds, so also is home-based learning proving attractive to older people. Some advantages are obvious: students do not need to wrestle with traffic; learning can take place whenever the student chooses. The disadvantages include being separated from the community of faith and missing interaction with other believers and seekers.

Individual Mentoring

Senior-to-senior mentoring is another pattern for studying and learning. Such mentoring may happen in small groups or even in larger classes where people meet with their peers. One interesting model encouraging such sharing of insights is the CAN-DO approach, discussed below. Congregations can readily adapt this idea.

A group of older people in an Ohio church organized a CAN-DO festival. Members of a church fellowship group for retirees wanted to know each other better. They also expressed interest in finding if there were skills or knowledge one person had that might be shared with others. At the CAN-DO festival, participants signed up to serve as mentors in their area of expertise. One man was willing to teach Spanish to another person or group. An elderly woman from Armenia offered to teach interested people how to play backgammon. Imagine her surprise when she learned that there was a man from Armenia who also wanted to play backgammon. Mentoring situations ranged all the way from sharing recipes to teaching others how to make stationery using pressed flowers.

Mentoring can be particularly effective when older church members agree to work with younger people such as confirmation students. Through sharing faith stories, the elder person communicates values and beliefs to those just beginning to explore religious truths. This is one of the approaches to intergenerational activities discussed in chapter 2.

Organized Classes

If your congregation has no structure for planning and administering adult education, it may be that interests of older adults will help bring such a structure into place. Although clergy or other staff may help initiate an appropriate planning group, they should not be actually designing and implementing curricula. Lay-led leadership for these tasks is essential. As Loren Mead has written, "Each congregation needs to be calling out teaching skills of more of its leaders so that the story of the faith is compellingly presented to the new and the long-term member, the young and the old."[2] Much informal learning occurs in any church or synagogue. Often this is the most effective and meaningful to the learner. However, there is also a place for more formalized learning experiences.

As an education committee or council meets, it will need to consider the following matters:

• survey of congregational interests
• course content
• prospective leadership
• time and length of courses

• location of courses
• promotion of courses
• evaluation

Surveying Needs

Any useful survey needs to be concise. In addition to listing possible categories (for example, Bible study or social issues), give examples of subtopics such as "Singing the Psalms" or "Who and Where Are the Homeless?" Provide opportunity for respondents to suggest topics. Set a deadline for returning the survey sheet, and be clear about where to return it. Sometimes it is better to distribute such forms at an already scheduled general meeting. Mailing surveys is both expensive and risky.

Determining Content

Study groups can range from being entirely unfocused and willing to explore any topic, to sticking rigidly with one subject and unwilling to accept anything extraneous. Each group will need to decide the degree of flexibility desired.

Possible areas for study are endless. Here are just a few examples of categories: spiritual growth (prayer, meditation, journaling); Bible study (topical approach, specific book of the Bible); ethical issues (advance directives, morality in the home); political matters (global or local); balancing body, mind, and spirit (exercise, nutrition, sleep); creative pursuits (gardening, painting, cooking). Analysts of congregations constantly remind us that many people coming into churches today bring no background in Christianity. From my own experience I know that this applies to older as well as younger people. One of the major tasks for every faith community is to study, study, study the roots as well as fruits of our beliefs.

Not only do denominations prepare useful materials for adult education, there are ecumenical centers such as The Alban Institute in Bethesda, Maryland, and Shepherd's Center in Kansas City, Missouri, that make significant resources available. Moreover, the National Interfaith Coalition on Aging in 1994 published *Incline Your Ear and*

Apply Your Mind to Knowledge.[3] This is described as a congregational resource book for locating, developing, and conducting services, programs, and activities for older adults.

Some congregations may want to explore "Discovery through the Humanities," a well-developed discussion series prepared by the National Council on the Aging. Program packets with creative materials for five to ten sessions include topics such as "The Search for Meaning," "The Heritage of the Future," and "Exploring Values."[4]

Locating Leaders

Each congregation has people with expertise in particular areas. These members, whether retired or still working, may welcome an invitation to share their knowledge and relate it to their faith. Women or men who have had eventful careers can draw on their experiences when leading discussions. An education committee is wise to begin collecting names of such people both within and outside of the congregation. Newspaper articles often highlight people with significant stories. Some former educators say they no longer want to play the teacher role. Consider asking them to be coaches for less experienced leaders. Do not overlook the wealth of people available through channels such as community colleges, media staff, nonprofit organizations, including Red Cross or area agencies on aging.

Time and Length of Courses

Although some small groups may want to continue indefinitely, usually participants prefer to know the length of time that a course will meet. Because many older people are reluctant to drive at night, it is desirable to schedule classes in the morning or afternoon. Sometimes half-day seminars are desirable—especially if such topics as living wills or managing home health care are being addressed.

Location of Courses

Classrooms in synagogues and churches appear to be the most common location for learning, but there are numerous alternatives to consider. "Home schooling" in later years could mean having retirees gather in a home, apartment, condominium—wherever members live—to share in growth groups. Current trends in church development indicate that small groups will be increasingly important as centers for nurturing the faith.

People can learn a great deal on field trips. Natural possibilities include visiting historic sites, nonprofit agencies (for example, centers for the blind or food banks), places of religious worship (temples, mosques, churches of other denominations), and local mission projects. Such activities obviously combine socialization and recreation with educational endeavors.

Daylong retreats or even overnight camps offer rich possibilities for continued learning. The expanded model described in Engaging Examples in this chapter presents information about a summer camp for seniors in Arizona. Almost all of the ideas can be adapted to other locations and time frames.

Promotion of Courses

In order to have successful education programs, it is important to make certain that potential students are aware of them. Here again, a Lifelong Learning Committee can take responsibility for promotion and publicity. Special mailings to prospective enrollees, registration tables, announcements in newsletters—all these and other creative approaches can motivate people to consider participation. If multiple classes are being held at the same time, indicate clearly where each course meets. For those who may have difficulty walking, specific instructions will spare them from going to wrong locations.

The committee may also want to promote valuable learning opportunities that are not sponsored by the church. Community colleges, hospitals, YMCA and YWCA organizations, health maintenance organizations, even shopping malls are eager to attract adult learners of all ages. As appropriate, consider encouraging clusters of people to enroll for the same classes. This can provide a basis for getting to know and sharing with each other. It may even prompt those who attend to modify ideas from the classes for use in their own congregation. Do not overlook the exciting world of Elderhostel, a popular movement offering courses on college campuses and numerous other locations around the world.[5] The success of this model proves that people age fifty-five and above are enthusiastic learners. Transferable suggestions from Elderhostel's impressive catalogs might spark responses from the committee.

Evaluation

Planners of educational offerings do well to prepare a simple evaluation tool for use at the end of a course. You may want to have a short checklist that addresses areas such as suitability of topic, location, methods used, new insights gained. Open-ended questions can also be helpful. Be sure to ask respondents to give ideas for future classes.

Engaging Examples

Camp 60—More or Less

Lay leaders in the Episcopal Diocese of Phoenix recognized the value of providing a church camp designed for older people. A prime mover in organizing Camp 60 was Bonnie Borden, R.N., who was on the staff of Episcopal Community Services in Phoenix. Through visiting many elders with health concerns, she became increasingly aware that these semi-isolated people were longing to be with others, to be out of their homes, and to keep learning. Additional members of the diocese plus leaders from other denominations developed plans that have remained workable for many years.

Camp 60, first held in 1985, has always promoted the following goals:

- provide a place where older people can enjoy making new friends
- offer stimulating study sessions
- interact with nature
- increase awareness of environmental issues
- strengthen personal faith

Camp 60 translates goals into action through the following kinds of activities:

Making New Friends

Although some people return each year with old friends, there are always first-time campers reaching out for new relationships. Friendships develop as people share cabins, participate in small discussion groups, eat meals together, play in the popular jug band, engage in afternoon activities, and have all the other informal contacts. Meals are intentionally a leisurely time when people can enjoy a second cup of coffee and engage in free-flowing conversation. Staff are sensitive to the needs of men or women who may seem to be having difficulty in relating to others.

Study Sessions

Each year the staff, often with suggestions from campers, selects a specific theme around which to develop programs. The morning study sessions are particularly focused on the stated theme. Here are examples of themes that have worked well:

- "On Wings of Faith" (the world of birds)
  Study periods incorporated the following subtopics:
     - God's Protection—Nests
     - God's Liberation—Wings
     - God's Guidance—Flight
     - God's Grace—Songs
- "Streams in the Desert—Sources of Living Water"
  Subtopics included:
     - Presence of Water
     - Preciousness of Water
     - Purification through Water
- "The Heavens Are Telling" (with special attention to astronomy)
  Subtopics included:
     - Creation (Genesis 1:1-5; Psalm 19)

- Incarnation (Matthew 2:1-12)
- Salvation (John 1:1-5)
- Dedication (Matthew 5:14-16)

Through the years a pattern has evolved such that each study session involves three components—usually presented by three different leaders. The first presentation highlights related elements of nature. Not only do campers learn about stars, rocks, birds, or whatever the emphasis, but they also discuss ways to be involved in environmentally related issues. The second presentation is a Bible study with passages closely related to the theme. Campers bring their own Bibles and during group time share interpretations of the Word. The third element is an application of the scripture passage to personal living. The leader for this segment prepares questions that are distributed to everyone. Singing and reading quotations from varied sources fill out the hour. After this plenary session and a break, each camper meets in his or her assigned small group where ideas from the opening hour are discussed in depth.

Interaction with Nature

For many older people, the opportunity to be out of doors is a rare, wonderful privilege. If weather is conducive to such activities as bird walks, stargazing through telescopes, or modest hikes to observe geological formations, that is ideal. Display tables and other types of exhibits invite further learning. Once the theme is announced, campers spend preliminary weeks, even months, gathering birds' nests, rocks, pictures of trees, or other examples of nature. Hearing authorities in areas such as astronomy or geology enriches the educational component.

Environmental Issues

In response to our role as stewards of God's creation, Camp 60 always tries to incorporate an ecological dimension. This helps learners move beyond the cognitive level to an action level. Thus, when focusing on "Streams in the Desert," the campers learned a great deal about water pollution and water conservation. Some even made posters describing ways to save water and to keep from polluting streams.

Many government agencies are eager to cooperate in providing information and special resources. For instance, when the camp theme was "The Tree of Life," the National Forest Service gave the camp large quantities of seedling pine trees. Campers could take them home to help in reforestation projects. Other natural connections between camp theme and environment include concerns about air pollution when studying birds, and soil conservation when studying rocks.

Strengthening Personal Faith

Participants recognize that Camp 60 is foremost a church camp. As such, it includes many ways to help campers reflect on God's presence. Each day begins with a morning meditation. This can be done privately wherever one chooses to go, or it can be shared with those gathering in designated places such as the rock chapel. Biblical passages that will be explored later in the day, plus classic prayers, are the central thrust of the printed meditations.

Music not only conveys fun but also expresses faith. Before the morning study time, campers gather to stretch and sing. Even the physical exercise portion celebrates the marvel of human bodies that are able to move and function. Each year people volunteer to sing in a choir. Their ministry of music contributes greatly to more formal worship experiences. Because this interdenominational camp is under Episcopal auspices, celebrating the Eucharist is very important.

Sharing faith stories is one of the most natural ways to nurture personal beliefs. This can happen in many settings: around the campfire, during meals, in small group discussions, through one-on-one conversations. Skilled leaders can often sense the teachable moments for encouraging faith reflections. A camp setting is ideal for this type of personal growth.

Each year this camp attracts approximately sixty participants. The majority of these are women, most of them widowed. Despite the name "Camp 60—More or Less," most campers range between seventy and eighty years of age. The actual ages of participants extend from twenty-six years to ninety-five. An interesting trend is that older adults are inviting their adult children to attend. One summer there were four sets of two-generation families.

About half the people enrolled are Episcopal; the rest are United Church of Christ, Methodist, Lutheran, Presbyterian, Roman Catholic, and Mormon. Although most of the staff attend Episcopal churches, some of the primary presenters are from other denominations. Most of these leaders are retired.

Originally, the camp met for only two nights. Those attending were so enthusiastic about their experience that they asked for a longer camp period. In more recent years the camp has run four days.

Because a camp setting offers opportunities for fellowship, growth in personal faith, a new environment, and recreation, it can meet the multifaceted needs of older people. Many of these same needs can be met in less elaborate settings, however. For instance, an overnight retreat can be very beneficial, especially if it is possible to be outdoors for part of it. There is no guarantee that new environments facilitate learning, but giving older people an opportunity to be more aware of sky, water, animals and other aspects of the natural world can increase their appreciation for God's creation. In some cases it may stimulate an earnest exploration of scientific study in areas such as astronomy, geology, and conservation. Even brief field trips can accomplish some of the goals embodied in Camp 60. If nature study is a primary interest, learning through media such as books and videos can be useful. Most congregations can easily obtain such materials.

Contact: Nancy Jo Carmichael, Director
Camp 60
2205 S. Wolverton Trail
Prescott, AZ 86303
(520) 445-6287

Bless Bible Studies: A Resource for Residents of Health Care Centers and Nursing Homes

In the 1980s, the Bible Study Task Force of the Nursing Home Committee of the Twin Cities Metropolitan Church Commission had an important vision. members determined that nursing home residents needed a curriculum designed specifically for their setting. Augsburg Publishing House published the resulting four-part series that addresses the following topics:

• Blessed by Jesus
• Blessed by the God of Abraham, Isaac, and Jacob
• Blessed by the Spirit
• Seasonal Studies

For each course listed above, there is both a leader guide and a book for participants. The leader guide includes useful insights about spiritual needs of residents, how to arrange and lead sessions effectively, tips regarding hearing and sight impairments, and a discussion of the importance of music. Each course has an audiotape with accompaniment for the suggested hymns. Leaders will find excellent resources described. Detailed instructions for developing each session help to make the material user-friendly. Hymns printed at the back of the guide are in clear, large print.

For participants, the format for each course is similar to that of the leader guide. There are twelve separate sessions. The theme for the day is clearly stated. For instance, in the course titled "Blessed by the God of Abraham, Isaac, and Jacob," individual sessions focus on themes such as "Caring for Others," "Listening to God," and "Waiting for God." The scripture passages become the basis for discussion. There is always a brief responsive sharing of Psalm 103, and the same blessing from Numbers 6:24-26 concludes each session. Such repetition is no doubt beneficial. In addition to a short prayer and ideas for meditation, there is a brief paragraph headed "Thinking It Over." That two- or three-sentence section summarizes the highlighted biblical passage and then invites students to ponder how the passage applies to their lives. Black and white photographs, many of them probably taken in nursing homes, may also enhance discussion.

This uncomplicated curriculum can be easily adapted for use in any situation where an older person is unable to attend adult education classes. According to Sally Frost, one of the writers for this resource, volunteers will find it easy to use. In facilities where there are chaplains or activities coordinators, they could appropriately supervise leaders who come in from the community to conduct the sessions. Used sensitively with an older population, *Bless Bible Studies* may prove to be a blessing to all who seek new insights from God's Word.

The series is no longer handled by Augsburg Fortress. Instead, contact:

St. Martin's Bookstore
2001 Riverside Dr.
Minneapolis, MN 55454
(612) 339-3920

Points to Ponder

1. What opportunities for learning does your congregation offer?

• general adult education
• education focused on older adults
• intergenerational education
• library
• specialized retreats or camps

2. Which offerings address the following:

• faith and belief issues
• social and political concerns
• matters of daily living
• skill building

3. What provisions do you have for equipping education leaders?

4. Which people or official committee members have responsibility for planning and evaluating educational events for your community of faith?

5. What are the resources in your community for lifelong learning?

6. How do you make members of your church or synagogue aware of these resources?

CHAPTER 4

Growing Down— Deepening the Roots of Faith

Growing Up—and Down

How many times when you were young did someone ask you, "What do you want to be when you grow up?" Usually you were expected to answer in terms of your desired profession or vocation. In an effort to help youth think about the answer to this question, some school districts have developed vocational guidance programs for students as young as elementary school age, in addition to the traditional programs for high school and college students.

In the context of our faith communities, we might consider posing another question. What are we becoming as we mature? How are our spiritual lives changing as we grow down? If our later years are unburdened by demands of job or parenting, we may discover new options for reflective living. The later years can truly be a time for deepening our awareness of God's presence.

"Growing down" does not imply "slowing down." Instead, it suggests sending out deeper roots into the soil of faith. Growing down also describes a process vital for focusing on gifts of the Spirit. I have always liked theologian Paul Tillich's understanding of God as "the ground of our being." In ministries with older adults, we seek ways to nurture those experiences designed to bring us closer to that ground of our being.

During several visits to Japan, I spoke with community leaders involved with their aging population. In various locations I asked a simple question: "What is the most important need of older people in Japan?" In the United States, older people's response to that question would probably include medical care, transportation, and economic security.

But respondents in Japan always said that their aging people need a meaning and purpose for living. That sounds like a search for an understanding of who we are becoming and why we are still alive. Such big questions lead us into the realm of the transcendent, into the arena of spirituality.

Spirituality Revisited

One result of the White House Conference on Aging in 1971 was the creation of the National Interfaith Coalition on Aging (NICA).[1] Leaders in NICA assumed the formidable task of defining spiritual well-being. For the last twenty-five years clergy and gerontologists have consistently cited that NICA definition: "Spiritual well-being is the affirmation of life in relationships with God, self, community and environment that nurtures and celebrates wholeness."[2] However, many of the same people who have quickly quoted that sentence now appear restless and ready to rethink the definition of spirituality in later years.

That human beings want meaning and purpose in life remains a paramount issue. Retired Baptist minister Robert E. Seymour writes in *Aging without Apology*, "No doubt a part of the reason older people turn to spirituality is to satisfy their search for meaning."[3]

For many people the very term *spirituality* seems amorphous and unthinkable, hard to imagine. In some respects we do not "think" our way into spirituality. The thinking dimension of being human connects us with powers beyond the realm of what is primarily physical. For Eugene Bianchi, author of *Aging as a Spiritual Journey*, the word *interiority* helps describe an inner awareness, an emotional climate that is part of our spiritual nature.[4] We cannot always measure such interior forces, but neither can we deny their reality.

As a journey suggests action and forward movement, so our growth in the spirit—the deepening of our soul—is a dynamic process. Age makes no difference. Contributors to the definitive handbook *Aging, Spirituality, and Religion*, comment on this process. "Focusing on nourishing souls represents a way of emphasizing a lifelong process rather than an end product."[5] Robert Atchley, professor of Social Gerontology at Miami University in Oxford, Ohio, emphasizes continuity as a theory connecting older people with their past.

The desire for continuity leads people to seek ways to express old values in new ways. Continuity of spiritual identity may become a more important goal for those who find that they have been immersed during middle adulthood in the secular aspects of their identity. . . . The spiritual self, especially if it is experiential rather than intellectual, may be less threatened by the infirmity and disability that sometimes comes with an advanced age. This is an additional motive for continuity of the spiritual self.[6]

Harry Moody, deputy director, Brookdale Center on Aging at Hunter College, New York, stresses mysticism as a key element of spirituality:

The mystical tradition provides the basis for a regulative ideal—a sense of purpose and meaning—for the last stage of life. . . . It may mean that attention to mysticism can open up new ways of thinking about what spiritual growth in later life might mean.[7]

How does this relate to the image of deepening our roots of faith by growing down? Such an image incorporates all we have said about continuity, interiority, transcendence, and even mysticism. It echoes a passage from Ephesians 3:14-19. In those verses the writer prays that the reader may be "rooted and grounded in love, may have the power to . . . know the love of Christ which surpasses knowledge, that you may be filled with all the fullness of God" (vv. 17-19).

Jane Thibault develops similar ideas in her book *A Deepening Love Affair*. She proclaims that the primary spiritual task for people in later life is to develop an intense, mutual love relationship with God. Insisting that life is a gift, she discusses why spirituality in later years can really be a celebration of giftedness.[8] Cultivating these gifts requires inner work in areas such as repentance and forgiveness, prayer, reading scripture, and entering into the passion of Christ. It necessitates helping young and old move into the "unthinkable" arenas of a Spirit world where we plumb the heart of God and respond to claims of the Holy One, our Creator. Are we in our churches ready to take on these tasks?

God's love is not changing, but the ways our churches and synagogues function must change. The *Once and Future Church* series published by The Alban Institute includes a book by C. Jeff Woods entitled

Congregational Megatrends. Among the seven megatrends he discusses is one that is particularly pertinent for this chapter. The author makes a strong case for the ways in which churches must move from a reasonable spirituality to a mysterious spirituality.[9] Although he did not write with particular attention to older people, I believe he can help us broaden our understanding of ways to fill later years with meaning and a sense of God's presence.

In *Aging without Apology,* Robert E. Seymour states that "the identification of spirituality with church activities is far too limiting. Genuine spirituality is never compartmentalized but permeates one's whole being."[10] If that is the case, just what role do religious institutions play to provide fertile soil and keep the roots of faith healthy?

Nurturing Spirituality in the Faith Community

Even though spiritual growth is an interior, personal process, to say that the church has no responsibility for enhancing this process would be a cop-out. Corporate worship, the heartbeat of church life, offers rich resources for necessary nurture. Key elements in services of the Word and Sacrament include scripture, hymns, prayer, sermon, and offering. Each of these suggests an area for individual growth.

Scripture

On any given Sunday morning across this nation, men and women gather for Bible study. Whether they worship in large cathedral-style church buildings or smaller simpler ones, members undergird worship with intentional study of the Word. For some, the sense of fellowship—just being with people who care about each other—may be more important than gaining theological insights. Yet even this sense of camaraderie is biblically based. It makes incarnate the body of Christ; it demonstrates how we can become members one of another (1 Corinthians: 12).

Content and method for Bible study vary. Although some curricula are written expressly for older people, I believe the main themes of the Hebrew scriptures and New Testament can speak to adults of all ages. For those congregations following the lectionary, study guides based on sermon texts can help classes interact creatively with the preaching. Many churches publish in advance the scripture references that will be used for the coming weeks, giving worshippers and class participants a head start in wrestling with the Word. Invite people to talk together about a passage; some older people may want to do this by telephone.

Of course, Bible study is not limited to Sunday morning; discussion groups often meet at times determined by members. In particular, older people often opt to meet during the day to avoid driving at night. Likewise, Bible study is not limited to a church building. Study groups meeting in homes may achieve a level of intimacy that might be less likely to develop in a more formal church setting. The study format is becoming more flexible as well. The teacher-centered, instructional approach familiar to most older learners seems to be giving way to more participatory approaches. Talking at students often proves to be less effective than engaging them in sharing their own thoughts and questions.

Maybe we do not challenge people enough to articulate their understandings of the Bible. My father was a minister in the United Church of Christ, ordained into the Congregational Church. Even though my father faithfully read the Bible, he and I seldom had intentional conversations about selected passages. As he grew into his eighties, he developed Alzheimer's disease. Still he found strength in rereading beloved sections of the Bible. One day, in preparation for a presentation I was making about the role the Bible can play in a person's later years, I asked my father if he would write out for me a list of scripture passages he turned to when he had particular needs. My mother worried that such an assignment would be too difficult for him, but eager to meet the challenge, my father labored long and lovingly. On his eighty-eighth birthday he presented to me his gift, reprinted in part here:

Bible Readings for Special Help in Personal Need

Prepared by Alexander S. Carlson, November 5, 1987 (eighty-eighth birthday)

- for peace in time of anxiety
  Psalm 4, Philippians 4:6,7
- for courage in time of fear
  Psalm 46, II Corinthians 4:4-18

- for comfort in time of sorrow
  Psalm 43, Romans 8:26-28
- for guidance in time of decision
  Psalm 32, James 1:5, James 5
- for relief in time of suffering
  Psalm 91, Hebrews 12:3-13
- for strength in time of temptation
  Psalm 1, I Corinthians 10:6-13
- for praise in time of thanksgiving
  Psalm 100, I Thessalonians 5:18
- for rest in time of weariness
  Psalm 23, Matthew 11:28-30

These categories make such good sense to me. My father's accomplishment stands as a good reminder that too often we underestimate abilities of the frail elderly, even those with dementia.

Hymns

I agree with an idea attributed to Martin Luther that next to the Bible the best resource for our devotional life is the hymnal. Men and women in their last decades of life, assuming they have grown up in the Christian fellowship, often cherish memories linked with hymns. Songs of faith not only engage the mind but also appeal to the emotions. Texts and tunes that are well matched capture our hearts and nourish our souls. But Jane Thibault raises this related concern: "I am convinced that our mainline Protestant and Catholic churches do not respond as well as they might to the hunger for spiritual experience that often emerges in the mature Christian. Our western culture is embarrassed by emotion."[11]

Making music with senior adults has delighted my whole being for nearly a quarter of a century. Since 1974 I have directed a choral group at the Beatitudes Campus of Care. We call ourselves the Beatitones; the average age of singers is eighty-four. Although we enjoy performing folk music, Broadway show tunes, and sing-along hits of yesteryear, the real favorites are hymns. Personal reflections surrounding treasured hymns often reveal spirit-filled experiences. In your setting encourage people to share their hymn stories.

If older people are lukewarm to church music, challenge them to give serious attention to words as well as music of both ancient and contemporary hymns. They may find new meaning by exploring stories of the poets and composers. Church libraries or public libraries usually have books presenting origins of hymns. One adult church class I visited in Fairfax, Virginia, used Patrick Kavanaugh's book *Spiritual Lives of Great Composers*.[12] Learning about the faith journeys of giants such as Johann Sebastian Bach, George Frederick Handel, or Ludwig van Beethoven can deepen one's appreciation of hymns that incorporate their music.

Because hymns cover the range of themes related to Christian living, they can be springboards for studying theology, Bible passages, and moods of prayer. No wonder many choir rehearsal rooms display posters with the message "Those who sing pray twice." Find innovative ways to use hymnals as catalysts for deepening roots of faith.

Prayer

"I've been going to church for seventy-three years, and I'm still not sure about this prayer business. How can God sort out the babbling in all the prayers' hearts?" This earnest question from a retired engineer reminds me that seasoned worshippers may still wonder about the power of prayer. For me, wonder itself is an element of prayer, perhaps the starting point for acknowledging God's presence.

Corporate worship experiences, embracing a variety of styles, usually include diverse attitudes of prayer. As older people review these attitudes, they may realize that they can continually come to God expressing praise and thanksgiving, confession, petition, intercession, and commitment. Every human need can relate to prayer.

The use of traditional prayers connects worshippers with the flow of history. Just realizing that believers and seekers through the centuries have longed for light and guidance may assure older members that modern struggles are not unique. Their ancestors also wrestled with despair, anxiety, and feelings of being abandoned.

Prayers of the people, sometimes called pastoral prayers, often include lifting up names of those who are ill as well as news about weddings, births, and deaths. One Sunday a beloved elder in our congregation commented to me, "When I hear that list read and know I'm not sick, I give thanks. It's comforting to know that if I am in the hospital or sick at home, you folks will be praying for me." During seminary days when preparing to lead chapel, I asked another student to review my drafted prayer. Words she wrote at the top of my paper have stuck with me: "Don't forget to pray! And I'll be praying for you." Inviting worshippers to pray for the person praying adds a deeper dimension of shared prayer life.

Sermon

When sermons retell the stories of God at work in our daily doings, we gain insights into who we are and who we might become. Again, praying for the preacher encourages those in the pews to engage actively in the preaching process. Feedback sessions after the service, especially if the preacher can be present, give responders a chance to formulate their own ideas. "I like to rework the words and try them out on other people," a thoughtful widow once told me. She often organized informal shared dinners in homes after church so people could react and interact to sermon ideas.

Offering

Have you ever heard a person on a limited pension say, "I can't afford to come to church anymore"? What a disturbing commentary on our understanding of worship. How can we help older people realize that what we bring to God includes more than money? The stewardship of time takes on new possibilities for those who are no longer regularly employed. In addition to tithes and offerings, we present our efforts on behalf of the homeless, we celebrate volunteer hours at a crisis nursery, we rejoice in serving God through mailing letters to legislators support-ing causes for peace and justice. Advocacy in the name of God can be a potent gift.

Celebrating the Sacraments

If we are cultivating mysterious spirituality, then participating in the sacraments becomes a truly holy time. Admittedly, diverse interpretations of Holy Baptism and the Lord's Supper too often drive Christians apart. Yet a sense of divine presence at communion reminds believers that God does work in mysterious ways. Are we surprised that senior church members may make extra efforts to join with others in celebrating the Eucharist, the great feast of thanksgiving? As one woman commented, "I don't get around much these days, but I make sure I have a way to get to the doctor, the supermarket, and church." That is quite a trinity to support health, wholeness, and spirituality!

Beyond Corporate Worship

In no way is spiritual growth confined to a sanctuary or any other formal place designated for worship. Candles, organ, and an altar are no guarantee that seekers will find themselves claimed by God's Spirit. Encountering the holy can happen any place, any time. We cannot emphasize this message too much. Early retirement years may bring a restlessness, an intensified desire to explore the world of the soul. Fresh approaches for pondering the presence of God keep springing up. Some of these approaches, including the use of crystals and numerology, reflect New Age ideas. Such practices may feed self-centered, narcissistic tendencies and never move beyond ego. A discussion with senior members about the New Age movement could be quite revealing.

Spiritual Life Retreats

A small group of people gathered in a quiet retreat setting may discover ways to encourage each other in spiritual journeys. The setting itself may not be so important. Just going to a neighboring church or private home introduces new possibilities. Sometimes by being out of our customary environments we listen more sensitively to inner thoughts and longings. Inspired by others who seek the sacred, retirees are often prompted to find time in their full schedules to be in retreat with other seekers. Events for reflecting on matters of the heart may be as brief as a half day or extend over several days.

Prayer Fellowship Groups

I Can Still Pray, written by Charles W. Peckham and Arline B. Peckham, is a bold title asserting that age makes no difference in communicating with God.[13] Indeed, older men and women disillusioned with cutthroat competition of the business world or tired of crass commercialism may yearn to find authentic pathways to meaning. Daytime prayer groups, gathering wherever is most convenient, can free participants to own their faith. Such groups flourish if they are nonjudgmental and willing to try new ideas.

Using a book such as *Beginning to Pray in Old Age* as a starting place may be less threatening to some than plunging directly into exposed soul-searching.[14] Genuine growth often happens more readily, however, when people risk sharing their inner joys and pains, sadnesses and celebrations. Nonordained people are sometimes more effective leaders than clergy, though clergy or staff can guide leaders to appropriate resources. Those who guide groups will want to emphasize how to cultivate the art of silence.

Prayer Partners

Praying with one other person can be a bridge to intimacy with self, other, and God. Such partnering can result from structured invitations extended through an official committee. Frankly, that sounds a bit sterile and impersonal. Yet when searchers do not know where to find a partner, it is better to have a formal clearinghouse rather than no means of connecting people.

If congregations describe the benefits of developing prayer partnerships, and if they provide resources, then people may find their own partners and launch a power-filled pilgrimage in prayer. These partnerships may take various forms:

• weekly sessions, perhaps in the home of one partner

- daily phone calls, including an unhurried listing of prayer concerns
- walking prayer partners: a "pray-as-you-go" approach that combines physical and spiritual exercising
- E-mail prayer partners using computers

Spiritual Direction

Seminaries and other centers for religious learning are returning to their role of equipping students for serving as spiritual directors. For those intensely interested in being equipped for inner growth and prepared to assist others in their quest, this opportunity bears investigating. See the address list in appendix A suggesting places to contact.

Leona, a retired university professor, had a lifelong love affair with the Episcopal Church. Thoroughly groomed in treasured traditions of her denomination, she kept feeling there was more to experience about the mysteries of resurrection faith. At age eighty, while recovering from a hip replacement, she decided to enroll in a two-year study program, "Contemplation in a World of Action." This course required reading, and understanding hefty theological terms, writing papers, and engaging in scholarly debate with younger students. Leona reported that although she wrestled repeatedly with ideas that challenged her more traditional beliefs, she relished the opportunity to clarify her thinking and grow in her spirituality.

Private Approaches

No one can ever do another person's living, learning, or listening to God. As we contemplate our own aging and perhaps frailty, thoughts about our mortality churn inside us. What a time, as well, for faith to surge through us. All kinds of gurus vie for our attention—and money— as marketeers ride the age wave. Several decades ago, Ken Dychtwald alerted us to this oncoming wave. In his book *Age Wave* he vividly describes the challenges and opportunities of an aging America. But he also acknowledges the last third of life as a time for personal reflection and growth in wisdom.[15]

Men and women in their later years can choose from a stimulating array of options on their preferred pathway to spiritual growth. Most of the elements in corporate worship discussed earlier—Bible study, hymns, prayers, offering of self—take on new meaning when used privately. Prayers and offering of self appear to be the most personalized. Workshops and seminars abound promising to teach meditation, imaging, visualization, Tai Chi, and other so-called self-help practices. Not all proponents have a religious orientation. If the goal is no deeper than *self*-help, then students may go away perhaps more relaxed or energized but not necessarily closer to apprehending the mystery of the eternal source of life.

Certainly we have much to learn from eastern religions, but a practice superimposed from someone else's belief system may not make much sense. Only when we claim the experience as our own can we sense the enveloping mystery at the center of faith. In our modern society of competing values and religions, so many spiritual vendors clamor for our allegiance. Jane Thibault's comment on this situation is a wise one.

> Be aware that there is no "good," "better," or "best" way to be in relationship with God. The important thing is for you to allow yourself to grow in conscious relationship. You may even experience different ways of being in relationship with God at different times in your life (even at different times of the day!) depending on your immediate need, life situation, physical health and emotional state, and needs of people in your life.[16]

Fruits of the Spirit

Roots lead to fruits. When we respond to God's love, we strengthen the best attributes of self and become empowered to share that love with God's other children. The gifts of the Spirit summarized in Galatians 5:22 are lifetime qualities that may assume even deeper meaning during the final years of life. Joy, peace, patience, faithfulness—such fruits nourish and sustain us when we face major transitions.

Donald Maldonado, professor of Church and Society at Perkins School of Theology, reminds us of the crucial role religious faith plays in the lives of many racial and ethnic minority leaders.

The sustaining power of these fruits applies to all God's family no matter what color or condition. The current generation of older racial and ethnic minority people, African Americans and Hispanics in particular, reflect high levels of religiosity including both private and personal dimensions. These people report that their religious faith and their churches aided them in coping with historical challenges to their well-being, and even today serve as critical resources for coping with the challenges of old age.[17]

The phrase "old age is not for sissies" has perhaps been overused, but there is an underlying truth that meaning-filled aging requires the cultivation of existing strengths. By not venturing into unknown territory we may feel safer, but we are deprived of the joys and risks of growth. In our Judeo-Christian faith, we believe God provides the courage we need to branch out in fresh ways. That same God nurtures us in later years as we risk deepening our roots of spiritual growth.

Engaging Examples

A Discovery in Prayer

A Disciples of Christ minister, together with members of a congregation he served in Oklahoma, developed a process to help people experience different types of prayer. Older people found this to be particularly meaningful. They describe the event, originally designed for a single meeting.

Divide participants into groups of about six to eight people. Have each group designate a leader. Explain that there are seven stations in clearly marked areas. The groups are to read and follow the instructions at each station. Every station has supplies and other necessary equipment such as Bibles, concordances, paper, pencils, thumbtacks, posterboard, and so forth. Announce that in an hour and a half there will be a ten-minute closing session.

At each of the seven stations located in different areas of the church fellowship hall, the following takes place:

1. Adoration and praise
Every person in the group suggests a passage of scripture and a praise song proclaiming the greatness of God. The group then selects one passage and one song and writes those on a sheet labeled "Adoration and Praise" at the first station.

2. Thanksgiving
The group reads together Ephesians 5:19-20. Each person offers a written or drawn example of why he or she is thankful for a particular sense: touch, smell, sight, hearing, or taste. Participants add the written or drawn response to the poster at station two.

3. Guidance
Have written copies of several prayers that deal with guidance. They may include various versions of the Lord's Prayer. Allow time for all to review the prayers. Then in pairs (determined by leader) talk about areas in own lives where guidance is most needed. Suggest that each person in the pair offer his or her partner a one-sentence prayer for guidance.

4. Confession
The group reads James 5:16 and discusses areas in which they need to be healed. They may also discuss problems related to confessing such need for healing. Those who are willing may share situations in which they are experiencing special needs for God's presence. Form a prayer circle at this station with open-ended prayer beginning "God, this is what I need." Those so inclined may write their need (with or without name) on the station four poster.

5. Intercession
Develop a prayer list with names of those the group wants to lift up in prayer. Names and needs may be put on individual cards and left in a prayer basket at station five.

6. Dedication
Sing together "Spirit of the Living God" (words available at station) and encourage all to ponder silently how they want God to melt, mold, fill, and use them. Have pipe cleaners, crayons, or clay available for those interested in fashioning a symbol to express how they will dedicate their

energies to God's glory. Either leave the symbols there or share them with the group at the closing session.

7. Reflection and summation

As time permits, invite people to share what they discovered about themselves and each other. The leader may guide group discussion with questions such as the following:

- Which form of prayer feels most natural for you? Which most difficult?
- How can we strengthen our understanding of the power of prayer for our congregation?
- In what ways might insights from this experience strengthen your private prayer life?

Instead of using six prayer concepts during one session, this approach might be done in several sessions, even six different gatherings. Rather than having people go through the stations in small groups, consider having people go through in pairs. Doing so might encourage more intimate exchange of ideas and feelings. A "stations of prayer" concept could well be adapted for a series during Lent.

Contact: The Rev. Richard Ziglar
Director of Northeast Active Timers
3817 S. Lewis St.
Tulsa, OK 74105
(918) 742-6826

Bible Explorations for Adults in Later Life

Laurie Sharpe, Director of the Third Age Ministry of the Cumberland Presbyterian Church Board of Christian Education, granted permission to reprint the following "Note to Participants" information. It introduces the Bible exploration materials available to congregations.

This six-part series explores scripture as it relates to concerns of people during later life. Each session is designed to last from forty-five minutes to an hour, depending on the amount of discussion generated by participants. Groups in the church might use this material for a six-week daytime discussion group or as a special series. Consider offering the series to homebound adults as individual study, and provide opportunities for sharing on a monthly basis in their homes.

The contributing writers have been asked to share their lifelong experience in relationship to the scriptures in their own words and in their own way through this resource. Each session addresses a concern on later life and takes a personal look at how the scripture has translated in the writer's life/ministry.[18]

The topics pertain directly to older people:

"Reviewing Life: A Task of Aging"
"Service: Job and His Message"
"Service: What Can We Do Now?"
"Dealing with Losses and Gains of Older Adults"
"Gaining a Wise Heart"
"Self-expression and Service Ministries"

This seventeen-page resource includes a brief sketch of each of the six older writers who prepared the materials. In addition to developing ideas about selected Bible passages, each contributor also prepared discussion questions. Knowing that the writers were laypeople and not professional, denominational staff brings, in my estimation, a sense of authenticity to the project. Materials written by peers, if prepared thoughtfully, often attract response.

Contact: Laurie Sharpe
The Cumberland Presbyterian Board
of Education, Third Age Ministry
1878 Union Avenue
Memphis, TN 38104
(901)388-1091

Points to Ponder

1. What does the phrase "growing down" mean to you? Discuss the phrase with older people in your congregation. What is their reaction?

2. Younger and older people have differing perceptions about the needs of elders. Ask people of varying ages, including those over age seventy-five, "What do you think are the greatest needs of older people?" Then directly confront retirees with the question, "What are *your* greatest needs?" Compare and contrast responses.

3. How does your congregation provide spiritual experiences, both thoughtful and mystical?

4. What provisions is your congregation making for older people to continue growing in knowledge of the Bible and to share their understanding of God's Word? You might invite people to compose their own list of treasured passages, similar to the list compiled by Alexander Carlson.

5. Hymns reflect many moods of prayer. Adult study groups may benefit from categorizing hymns in terms of the following prayer themes: adoration, thanksgiving, confession, petition, intercession, commitment.

6. To which informal venues for spiritual growth do older people in your congregation seem most attracted? Why?

CHAPTER 5

Serving and Being Served

Volunteering—An Expression of Belief

"Do you mean that these retired people actually work without getting paid?" Hans, a young adult from Germany who asked this question, had come to the United States to learn how churches use volunteers. Again and again he expressed amazement as he saw sights such as:

- a former schoolteacher driving a van to take a group of widows shopping
- a retired secretary typing letters for a pastor
- a man in his nineties tutoring teenagers at a neighborhood center
- a woman legally blind answering telephone calls in a synagogue office
- a group of men devoting one day a week to constructing ramps for mobile home residents who use wheelchairs

Although these are not particularly dramatic scenes, they represent thousands of stories repeated across the nation. Older people donate millions of hours each year serving in a multitude of capacities. The largest single category of institutions using volunteers are faith-related organizations, including churches and synagogues.

Our Judeo-Christian religion instructs us to care about other people and all creation. Loving God, neighbor, and self is a theme that permeates the Bible. Stories from the Hebrew Scriptures portray men and women constantly interacting. David and Jonathan help each other; Miriam and all the other women of the Exodus play tambourines and dance. In the New Testament a multitude of eager listeners sitting on a hillside share their lunches. Mary and Martha offer hospitality in their home. No one worries about keeping a list of volunteer hours, yet in a very real sense the biblical story chronicles acts of charity as responses to God's love.

Marlene Wilson, internationally acclaimed authority in the field of volunteerism, discusses the theology of volunteering. In *How to Mobilize Church Volunteers,* she writes:

> When we talk about learning how to mobilize people in our churches, it is essential that we pause before getting into the "how-tos" and deal seriously with the "whys." That's really what theology is—the why behind our beliefs and actions. And that is exactly where the church *is* and *must be* different from any other organization. We must be clear about our reasons for both being and doing, or church work becomes just another activity to squeeze in (if we must) or get out of (if we can).[1]

I doubt that many people who prepare meals in homeless shelters or read mail to residents in nursing homes consciously formulate theological statements about their motives, yet we do well to help people see the connection between their belief systems and resulting actions.

Other Motives for Volunteering

Volunteerism is often seen as a way of life for those of us living in the United States. Since my youngest days I have been aware of options for volunteering. Whether I was singing in junior choir or walking a neighbor's dog, playing the piano for residents at a nursing home or writing a skit to promote the church building fund, I had choices for investing my time. Moreover, I felt that what I chose to do was important.

"Make a difference." That phrase occurs repeatedly in literature related to volunteerism. Although the subtitle of another Marlene Wilson book is "Helping Others and Yourself through Volunteering," the title is *You Can Make a Difference*. The colorful cover for *Acting on Your Faith* by Victor Claman and David Butler includes the subtitle "Congregations Making a Difference." Knowing that their efforts are significant is important to volunteers.

Reasons for volunteering usually include the following:

• We want to make a difference in the lives of others.
• We view the opportunity as one way of expressing our faith.
• We need ways to combat loneliness.
• We feel the cause is important.
• We long for self-esteem and affirmation.
• We like the group of people involved in a given project.
• We have talents, insights, and experience to share.
• We learn new skills and information.

Seasoned Volunteers

The motives listed above can apply to people of any age, but some of them take on special meaning when pertaining to older adults. Paul Maves' book *Older Volunteers in Church and Community* was one of the first to concentrate on this topic.[2] He cites impressive reasons why older volunteers are different. One significant difference is that they have more discretionary time. Yet we often hear retirees say, "I have never been so busy." Sometimes they convey exasperation; other times they are proud, even boastful. Because older people are often involved in numerous activities, we need to be flexible in using their services.

Another difference seasoned volunteers bring is their wealth of past experience. This experience includes not only professional accomplishments but also personal ones such as rearing families and developing avocations. Although wisdom is not automatically a byproduct of living longer, many of our elders have developed a clear sense of values and judgment.

Maves reminds readers that older people may have physical changes requiring modifications in their assignments.[3] If an assigned responsibility is outside the home setting and the volunteer no longer drives, another volunteer must provide transportation. Jobs requiring manual dexterity, even as simple as putting mailing labels on envelopes, may cause pain for fingers gnarled by arthritis. One way to avoid frustration for everyone is to gather facts about each volunteer including any limitations on time, location of activity, and physical requirements.

Cultivating Volunteers—The "I's" Have It

Many resources outlining needs of volunteers address the importance of recruiting, retaining, and recognizing those men and women who agree to serve. When reviewing ideas from several authors, I became aware that primary principles could be related to words beginning with the letter *i*. Open your eyes to what these "i's" propose.

Invite

How do older people know that you have needs for their services? Find creative ways to publicize your openings. Most churches make steady use of newsletters, public announcements, and personal invitations. The latter approach is probably the most significant, especially if the tasks require expertise of a technical or relational nature. We ultimately create problems for ourselves if we invite everyone, then discover that some who responded are not appropriately qualified for the job. Nobody likes to uninvite a willing respondent. But don't forget—there are ways to reassign volunteers.

Interview

How do you know if the job and person are right for each other? Before orienting volunteers, you will want to learn more about their back-grounds and interests. Application forms can include pertinent information such as routine personal identification, past work and volunteer experiences, hobbies, other community involvements, and any other questions that help you gain useful insights. Recognize that retirees often juggle complex schedules, and be sure to document preferred times for working including time of day, days of week, and anticipated travel plans.

Inform

What information do volunteers need before starting their assignments? Be sure to provide clear job descriptions. Older people may have diminished eyesight or hearing loss. Write instructions clearly and in reasonably large print. Whether their task is trimming bushes or creating decorations for a banquet, volunteers like to know how their efforts relate to the larger picture. Discuss the importance of the job.

Interact

What if volunteers become discouraged or even disgusted? Continuing support is a key to successful volunteer programs. If a homebound woman is mailing cards to church members in the hospital, call her to share any feedback related to her efforts. Some people prefer to be left alone; they treasure freedom to develop assignments as they see fit. The more awareness you have of volunteers' abilities, the more you may be able to let them function on their own. But to abandon volunteers is to court disaster.

Invest

How can we let volunteers know that we appreciate their contributions? Not all workers want public recognition. Most people, however, like to know that they are doing a good job. Print names in publications, write notes expressing appreciation, telephone to say "well done." Thank volunteers again and again. Some churches periodically celebrate through brunches or picnics. Even though such events require time and money, they are priceless investments.

Interpret

Why is evaluation important? Some volunteer tasks, such as designing stewardship campaigns, recur periodically, perhaps annually. Reviewing outcomes with the volunteer may lead to revising procedures. Perhaps even more important is the opportunity for the volunteer to share feelings about the assignment, expectations, and results. If someone wants to retire from a volunteer position, explore reasons for that person's request. Although certain volunteers prefer to stick with the same job year after year, others want variety. This may be especially true for young retirees investigating various types of opportunities. Pressuring people to remain when they are unhappy is usually counterproductive. Document evaluation sessions so that you can interpret and learn from each experience.

Preferences in Volunteering

Freedom of choice is one of the major attractions of volunteering. Note the wide range of decisions that older people face when exploring volunteer options.

Time Commitment

- regular hours on a scheduled basis (weekly or monthly)
- flexible hours as determined by volunteer
- episodic (time-limited involvement)
- full time—brief engagement for a week or two
- full time—extended for three months to several years

Location

- at home (such as addressing envelopes or designing program covers)
- at church or synagogue (inside or outside)
- in local community
- beyond local community (regional, national, or global)

Nature of Assignment

- task-oriented (with others or alone)
  (see special categories listed below)
- person-oriented (with others or alone)—children, youth, young adults, adults, seniors, people with disabilities, people confined to home

Specific Arenas for Volunteer Services

This list will vary from congregation to congregation. Develop an awareness and list of responsibilities that do not require staff involvement. As churches come to realize that all members are commissioned to be in ministry, then the possibilities for enlisting volunteer support become almost endless. Volunteer positions may be classified under these broad categories (only a few examples are given for each category):

- Worship (sing or play in choirs, greet, usher, work on altar guild, participate as liturgist)
- Education (teaching, library, field trips, retreats)
- Caring (visitation, phoning, transportation, letter-writing)
- Administration (planning, executing events, promoting)
- Advocacy (research on social issues, speaking in church or community, contacting decision makers)
- Support service (data entry, painting, preparing food, gardening, housekeeping)

Volunteer Choices for Homebound Older Adults

When men and women are no longer able to be physically active, they may no longer feel useful. Feelings of uselessness bring up dilemmas of personal worth based on productivity, a topic discussed later in this chapter. There are, however, meaningful ways that less physically able members may contribute. Add your own ideas to this list.

- Review books for the church newsletter.
- Telephone isolated people.
- Be a pen pal to a child.
- Cut stamps for mission projects.
- Send cards to members in hospitals.
- Assist in recording history of church.
- Continue or learn skills including knitting, painting, word processing.

Opportunities beyond Local Congregation

Although every congregation usually has numerous opportunities for engaging members in volunteer roles, there are also significant ministries in the wider community. Social agencies, both public and private, steadily appeal for help. Sometimes clergy and other church staff complain when their members volunteer in hospitals, prisons, shelters, scouting programs, adult day care programs—any institutions or missions requiring dedicated service. Yet, these are all avenues for ministry. Why not applaud those who put into action the messages of faith? Some churches even celebrate during worship the ways in which members respond to social ills by taking seriously the commands to work for peace and justice.

What about opportunities to help in locations beyond one's immediate vicinity? Many denominations sponsor work camps or other kinds of volunteer placement. For years the Presbyterian Church (U.S.A.) has offered their Volunteers in Mission (VIM) program designed to match skills of younger and older people with needs of denominational institutions. This service experience, which lasts from several months to a few years, often results in enduring friendships.

Beyond denominational structures are enticing alternatives such as national projects for Habitat for Humanity, Red Cross, Volunteers in Service to America (VISTA), and the Peace Corps. All of these welcome eligible people in their later years. A national program focused on those age sixty or over is the Retired Senior Volunteer Program (RSVP). More than a half-million retirees participate in 760 project service areas located throughout the nation.

Faith communities can learn a great deal from the Elderhostel success story. What started on a shoestring at the University of New Hampshire in 1975 has blossomed into a worldwide network of dynamic older learners. Nearly a quarter of a million people study and travel every year under Elderhostel auspices. In 1992 Elderhostel Service Programs began. Opportunities include building affordable houses in poor American communities, teaching English in eastern Europe, and counting endangered sea mammals in the Caribbean. The combination of learning and serving appeals to thousands of people over age sixty. Human needs abound; skills and talents among retired men and women also abound. We must continue to design ways to match the needs and gifts.

To Serve and Be Served—Beyond Autonomy

Although people—including those in their eighties and nineties—may be eager to tell how they are helping others, they may be very reluctant to accept help from others. Practicing in the field of gerontology for decades, I have become acutely aware of ways our society glorifies the concept of independence. Look carefully at advertising for long-term care facilities and you will see that they repeatedly emphasize ways they help people remain independent. Who will help people learn to be inter-dependent?

Churches and synagogues may organize teams of volunteers, but even elderly who need transportation or shopping services may insist, "I can do it myself." Of course, there is the risk of that notion that people have the right to refuse help, even if it becomes detrimental to their safety. The god of autonomy rules many lives in our culture where self-reliance still dominates.

One congregation devoted a year of programming to issues challenging older adults. When confronting topics of hearing loss, they featured a group of signers who made no apology for deafness. In study sessions, members of the congregation discussed ways they were coping with various types of limitations. Some of them confessed their frustration, even anger, at having to accept help. That help included using adaptive devices as common as hearing aids or canes.

Is our dread of seeming to appear less than whole a reflection of our unwillingness to admit our mortality? This is a big theological question that deserves serious attention. Pushed to the extreme, our insistence on doing everything for ourselves means we have no need for God. We are totally self-sufficient. That, I think, is a dangerous heresy. One way to combat this heresy is to model for others our willingness not just to serve but also to be served.

Engaging Examples

We can only hope that illustrations of service abound in every congregation. Some projects may be tailored to internal needs, such as assisting with clerical or maintenance functions of the church. On another level, service may be designed and organized to involve several churches and

synagogues working together. This model often works well for programs
such as shelters for the homeless or advocacy for people with AIDS. As
mentioned earlier, some projects have national affiliation. The success
of this model is well illustrated by disease-oriented organizations such
as the American Cancer Society or the National Alzheimer's Association.

National Federation of Interfaith Volunteer Caregivers, Inc.

In 1984 the Robert Wood Johnson Foundation funded twenty-five communities who applied for funds to establish Interfaith Volunteer Caregivers groups. This three-year pilot project proved the value of having
congregations cooperate to organize volunteers to help meet the needs of
people who are chronically ill, homebound, or living with disability. On
a neighbor-to-neighbor basis and under the direction of a paid staff coordinator, volunteers of all ages provide help with shopping, respite,
transportation, home repairs, personal care, meal preparation, and other
tasks that allow individuals to stay in their own homes.

In 1993 additional funding from the Robert Wood Johnson Foundation established the Faith in Action program granting technical assistance and start-up financial support to faith communities that want to
launch volunteer programs. By 1996 there were six hundred interfaith
caregiving groups functioning across the nation.

Interfaith Caregivers, Inc. of Olean, New York

A good example of the Faith in Action program is the Interfaith Caregivers, Inc., in Olean, New York. As one of the original groups organized in 1984, this project functions effectively in a small community
(population of 17,000) and surrounding rural area. Although the fifty
participating congregations are predominately Christian, there is one
Jewish synagogue and volunteers who are Muslim and Hindu.

What do the three hundred volunteers do? In addition to providing
traditional caregiving services such as shopping, transportation, and
respite assistance, participants meet special requests including sewing,
electrical repairs, and help with insurance bills. Driving people to

medical treatments can require many hours. For example, those living in nonurban areas may have to travel at least one hundred miles one way to receive kidney dialysis. Volunteers not only do the driving, they also wait many hours while the person receives treatment.

Leadership in Olean consists of three full-time staff members, two half-time workers, and numerous office volunteers. Although some Interfaith Volunteer Caregivers programs prefer to have designated co-ordinators in each congregation, the Olean project has a different ap-proach. People needing help—and the majority of them are over age sixty-five—call the office. The Volunteer Coordinator matches the request with an available volunteer who has agreed to perform the needed service. Because people usually prefer to serve in areas where they already have experience, the Olean model does not require that volunteers attend an orientation session.

Both those serving and those being served are most often of retire-ment age. The largest single age category of Olean recruits is between the ages of sixty and seventy-four. Those over age seventy-five consti-tute the second largest age group. There is even a volunteer who at age 101 was making daily phone calls to frail elderly men and women.

No matter how large or small a congregation may be, volunteer ministries can be a vital way to put faith into action. By combining ef-forts with other congregations, churches and synagogues can have an impact on communities with needed services and with a demonstration of the power of loving, caring neighbors.

Contact: Joan R. Wells, Executive Director
Interfaith Caregivers, Inc.
P.O. Box 319
Olean, New York 14760
(716) 372-6283

Senior Resource Coordinator

"To link seniors in our congregation and community with services they are entitled to, and to assist their families as well"—that is the stated purpose of a volunteer program known as Senior Resource Coordinator. The Community of Congregations, a coalition of churches in the region of Oak Park, Illinois, received a modest grant from the Retirement Research Foundation to launch an innovative project. The ramifications of this idea are far-reaching, yet the design is so simple that congregations could implement this program with little or no expense.

A Senior Resource Coordinator (SRC) is an older unpaid staff person who donates eight to ten hours per week on behalf of his or her peers. Chosen by clergy or other staff, the SRC is a respected member of the congregation capable of referring members to needed services.

Florence Pogue, member of a Disciples of Christ Church in Oak Park, writes enthusiastically of her role as a Senior Resource Coordinator.

> The pastor of my congregation allows me to use the space I need in the church, and he prints 'Florence's Corner' in our biweekly newsletter as a service to members. Once a week I have office hours at the church and make myself available to those who require my services. I am equipped with resource directories, and if I need additional information, I can always call those who are paid staff in their particular area.
>
> I have a lot of telephone contact with older church people and their families as well as community providers. Part of my task is to keep searching for new information and updating existing data. I really keep busy, and I thank God that I am able to help. I don't complain about being busy as it is so much better than doing nothing with my gifts.

Based on my own experience, I realize that when trying to help people locate information about needed services we can spend huge amounts of time. By identifying the right volunteer to serve as resource coordinator, the church staff, not just the inquirer, will benefit.

Contact: Florence Pogue, Senior Resource Coordinator
Austin Boulevard Christian Church
634 N. Austin Boulevard
Oak Park, IL 60302
(708) 386-5664

Points to Ponder

1. From your experience, what do you think are the major reasons why people volunteer their time and talents? In what areas do *you* volunteer? Why?

2. How does your congregation express appreciation to volunteers? What additional ways might you consider?

3. Make an inventory of tasks in your congregation performed by volunteers. Which tasks are older people performing?

4. When people join our congregations, we are usually eager to "put them to work." How do you assess new members' talents and interests and then communicate that information to appropriate contact people?

5. In what ways are you reluctant to accept help from others? Ponder the theological dimensions of these two extreme attitudes: "I am totally helpless—no good—unable to do anything for myself or others." "I am totally independent; I don't need help from anyone."

6. Many older people are putting their faith into action by serving needs in the wider community. How can churches and synagogues encourage and celebrate this type of involvement in those worthy agencies?

CHAPTER 6

Letting Go and Growing in Faith

Choices about Changes

As we accumulate birthdays decade after decade, we notice changes in our bodies and in the world around us. Have you ever attended a high school or college class reunion? If so, you have probably reflected on how classmates retained certain characteristics but in other ways seemed to be different. Often we first notice external changes such as balding heads, graying hair, trifocal glasses, and probably some extra pounds. By the fiftieth or sixtieth class reunion, we may well be showing signs of slowing down.

Ideas about aging that developed during this century include the disengagement theory that implies that aging people will gradually withdraw from social involvements. In opposition to that rather negative view are insights from Lydia Bronte, author of *The Longevity Factor*. She insists that as people are living longer they are also remaining productive in their careers that may extend to at least age seventy-five.[1]

There is some truth in the adage "Aging is a matter of mind over matter: if you don't mind, it doesn't matter." Attitude can certainly influence how one lives out the final years. Over and over I have heard elderly friends quote the prayer attributed to Reinhold Niebuhr: "God grant me the serenity to accept what I cannot change, the courage to change what I can, and the wisdom to know the difference." One cigar-smoking octogenarian quipped, "But who has that sort of wisdom?"

Changes do occur in later years. A loss such as death of a spouse can threaten to drive the survivor to despair. Forced retirement may lead to bitterness. I knew a woman in her mid-sixties who had risen to the position of chief executive officer in a health care facility. She was proud of her accomplishments. She gave out her business card at every opportunity. Shortly after her mandatory retirement she moaned, "I don't have any letterhead that says who I am!" Such loss of self-esteem is tragic. How can congregations help members deal with losses and feelings of worthlessness?

Symbols of Selfhood

An activity I call "Symbols of Selfhood" takes an interesting approach to addressing attitudes toward aging. You can adapt it for use with groups of pre-retirees, recent retirees, frail elderly, or relatives in a younger generation. It could even be done on a one-to-one basis. First, gather significant symbols of personhood such as a mirror, set of keys, birthday card, dollar bill, newspaper, shoes, or other clothing that suggest physical activity. Then ask participants to comment on the importance of each item for their daily lives. Keeping in mind the ages and situations of those in the group, talk together about how the meaning of these symbols might change as people grow older.

When using this process with older people, I have noted that usually the conversation moves to the concept of independence versus dependence. Anxieties emerge about not being able to drive a car or not appearing young. The dollar bill leads to comments regarding worries about financial stability. When contemplating the newspaper, one teacher mentioned, "I'm afraid I might lose my eyesight. My mother had such terrible problems with macular degeneration." Tennis shoes prompted thoughts about decreasing activity, arthritic joints, apprehension about giving up a bowling league.

On the surface these may sound like insignificant topics, but they represent deep concerns shared by so many in later years. Churches and synagogues have the opportunity to demonstrate how faith in God's eternal goodness can support members who experience losses in later life. What would happen if a group of older people identified their own symbols of hope? Would they include the Bible? Can the same symbols associated with letting go also be associated with growing in faith?

Living with Losses

Women from a Presbyterian church in northern Arizona asked me to
lead an autumn retreat dealing with the theme "Letting Go." They
wanted to consider not only the changing seasons of nature but also the
changing seasons in human lives. Planners asked, "As we grow older
how can we deepen our faith even as we let go of parts of life?" As I
prepared for the retreat I recognized at least three aspects needing attention: letting go of relationships, activities, and things we have accumulated. Arranged in reverse order—things, activities, relationships—
I suddenly recognized the acronym TAR. Getting stuck in warm tar is
no fun; getting stuck in the past with an unwillingness to let go is also
dis-tressing. Yet, our "stuckness" need not be hopeless.

Letting Go of Things

The phrase "You can't take it with you" has fresh meaning for people
who pile up possessions year after year. When children grow up and
maintaining the family home becomes burdensome, older people may
want to move to smaller quarters. "But what will I do with all this
stuff?" becomes a familiar lament. Don Aslett's book *Clutter's Last
Stand* combines wit and wisdom about dealing with the heaps of things
in our lives.[2]

   Those who downsize their living space wonder not only which possessions to relinquish but also what to do with them. At this point faith
communities may provide useful guidance.

- Publicize reputable charities that operate thrift stores.

- Encourage downsizers to give special possessions to family members
  or friends who will treasure the items.

- Create a home benediction ritual that can offer a faith-centered clo-
  sure to a dwelling that may be filled with powerful memories.

- Provide programs that include demonstrations of how to preserve
  precious documents, pictures, and recollections of the past. Find

experts who know techniques for recording life experiences as well as those who can teach ways to maintain important papers.

Giving up a car can be a traumatic experience. Our mobile society lives on wheels. Teenagers urgently await the day when they will acquire their driver's license, their ticket to independence. Relinquishing a license often causes anguish for the former driver. What can be done?

- Counsel at-risk drivers who stubbornly refuse to stop driving.

- Organize volunteers to provide transportation for church and synagogue activities and perhaps for medical or other important appointments.

- Arrange brief or longer excursions for those no longer able to drive.

- Help former drivers learn about alternative modes of transportation such as bus service or public door-to-door provisions.

- For those older people still behind the wheel, promote refresher courses such as "Fifty-five Alive" developed by AARP.

- Assist people in focusing on what remains, not just what is gone.

We need to anchor our ideas about reducing material goods in a theological discussion regarding life's priorities. What are the enduring qualities of being alive? How do we confront contemporary society's emphasis on consumerism? What produces pat rack mentality? What are today's golden idols (see Exodus 32) and who is marketing them? How do we interpret Jesus' message "For where your treasure is, there will your heart be also" (Matthew 6:21)?

Letting Go of Abilities and Activities

Textbooks abound on the physiology of aging. Medical researchers continuously study cell structure and genetic complexities seeking to understand why and how we age. Remarkable scientific breakthroughs shed significant light on ways to keep bodies functioning at maximum efficiency. Yet no one asserts that we are immortal. Cell structures change with the years. We accommodate diminished eyesight or hearing by using glasses and hearing aids. Those experiencing problems with mobility have an almost endless choice of aids, from simple canes to electric scooters. Coping with loss of memory causes frustrations for anybody who experiences it. Fortunately, the Alzheimer's Association has excellent resource materials and guidance directed primarily to the caregiver.

All ages can advocate "user-friendly" church and synagogue buildings. Determine how do your facilities measure up regarding the following:

Communication

- large-print copies of hymns, prayers, liturgies, newsletters
- sufficient lighting for congregation and worship leaders
- adequate sound system
- sermons or entire services on audiotape
- printed copies of sermons

Physical Space

- designated parking for people with handicaps
- accessible entrances by ramps
- wide and easily opened doors
- adequate space in worship area for wheelchairs and people who need extra leg room
- accessible bathroom(s)

For specific guidelines contact the National Organization on Disability or the Healing Community (see appendix A for addresses).

Underlying our reactions to changes in bodily functions is our fear of losing control. I believe our society has overrated the acclaimed goal of individual autonomy. As youngsters, when mastering tasks such as

tying our shoes, we took pride in announcing, "I can do it by myself."
But God has created us to be not independent but interdependent.

As a composer I often weave original songs into my preaching or
public speaking. One jazzy creation always seems to strike a responsive
chord in the listeners. The lyrics include this verse:

> I can do it by myself—*(pause)* maybe.
> I can manage without help—*(pause)* maybe.
> Independent to the end,
> I don't even need a friend.
> I can do it by myself—*(pause)* maybe.[3]

Pushed to a logical conclusion, our insistence on total autonomy
means we have no need for God. Any concept of a savior is meaningless.
Insisting that all we need is to "pull ourselves up by our own bootstraps"
smacks of religious heresy.

My own experiences of grappling with limitations resulting from
polio helped me realize two extreme reactions to physical losses. One
attitude is that of totally denying any bodily change and insisting "I can
do everything by myself." We see that denial acted out by people who
refuse to use aids such as walkers, magnifying glasses, or Depends.® On
the other hand, people may assume a posture of complete helplessness,
unwilling to take responsibility for any of their actions. That attitude
contributes to defeatism, the syndrome of lying around mumbling, "I
can't do anything."

Letting Go of Relationships

Although a sense of grief may accompany any loss, including the loss of
things and abilities, it may be most acute when the loss involves human
relationships. R. Scott Sullender, Presbyterian minister, counselor, and
family therapist, addresses this matter in his book *Losses in Later Life:
A New Way of Walking with God.*[4] The author discusses not only the loss
of spouse, often the most stressful loss, but also the loss of parents and
the loss of family. No congregation is without members grieving losses
through death, through alienation such as divorce, and through separation, as when family members move to another part of the country.

Listing the types of relational losses afflicting people in your church or synagogue can prove helpful. If this is done within an intimate group, such a listing will reveal the level of knowledge that members have about one another. The phrase "when we care we are aware" reminds us that our depth of caring may reflect our depth of awareness. This is an area in which older adults often excel. Encouraging the sharing of pastoral concerns helps members know that they each have a role in the caring ministry.

Here are categories of severed relationships that may require compassionate intervention.

Loss of Professional "Authorities"

This includes the death, retirement, or moving away of lawyer, physician, dentist, chiropractor, counselor, beautician—any human service personnel with whom special bonds have been developed. Pastors, priests, and rabbis also belong in this category. If such professional or paraprofessional people have served as confidantes, the loss may be magnified. To reassure the grieving person that "you will find another doctor" is to ignore the pain of the moment and symbolically reject the sorrowing person.

Loss of Older Family Members

Because our life expectancy has increased dramatically during the twentieth century, it is not at all unusual for families to have two generations of relatives in retirement years. Adult children in their sixties and seventies care for their aging parents, aunts, and uncles. When the most aged relatives die, those in the next tier realize that "now we are the oldest generation in our family," a stark reminder of our mortality.

Sullender observes that "the loss of parents is a difficult loss for many adults because its grief is largely ignored and undervalued in our society. The grief that adults feel when their parent(s) die is a secret grief . . . that millions of adults carry around with them year after year."[5]

Loss of Younger Family Members

Surviving the death of a child brings agony at any life stage. When elderly parents suffer the loss of an offspring, they may question why those who are younger die before those who are older. As in any grief situation, we may compound pain by trying to give easy answers.

Death is not the only source of separation. Hostilities, unresolved conflicts, divorce—all these contribute to loss of relationship between older and younger generations. In a society where an alarmingly high percentage of couples divorce, the shaking of the family tree affects all the branches. Contact with grandchildren may change. With blended families there are new challenges to retain a sense of rootedness.

Loss of Pets

For some older people their deepest bond may be with a cat, dog, or other pet. When considering moving from home to an institutional setting, the first question some applicants ask is "Can I bring my pet?" For those living alone, the presence of an animal provides a vital source of meaning. Even having to care for winged, finned, or four-legged friends can justify getting up each morning. Grief following the death or removal of a companion animal should not be minimized.

Responding to Relational Losses

How many ways are there to respond to personal losses? Probably as many ways as there are individuals struggling through those losses. The word *resilience* does not appear in my Bible, but the concept permeates the scriptures. We preach and teach about love and about hope. Men and women recently widowed repeatedly find strength in passages such as Psalm 23 (walking *through* the valley of the shadow of death), Psalm 90 (easily associated with Isaac Watt's hymn "O God, our help in ages past, our hope for years to come") and Romans 8:39 (nothing "will be able to separate us from the love of God in Christ Jesus our Lord"). By enfolding and upholding survivors with such ageless truths, we do empower them to become resilient.

But how do we minister to those with losses who are also suffering depression?

- Peer counseling utilized in some senior centers can be a model for congregations. Active listening requires skill and patience, yet these skills can be learned.
- Grief support groups under sensitive leadership enable participants to share pains and joys. It is hoped that those who attend will be able to resume normal activities within a reasonable length of time.
- Physical activity can be therapeutic. Walking or swimming, for example, especially when shared with others, restores vigor to body, mind, and spirit.
- Help members of the congregation keep in touch with those who mourn. Prolonged isolation can drive humans to self-destructive behaviors through use of such chemicals as alcohol and prescription drugs. If churches are the body of Christ, then all parts of the body need to be in communication. Phone calls, home visits, shared meals, study and prayer groups—all are potential sources of healing and wholeness for those in grief.

Additional Losses

In addition to dealing with the loss of things, activities, and relationships, many people get stuck in the loss of dreams and youth. Now our acronym becomes TARDY. Relinquishing certain dreams does not mean the end of dreaming. Yet, too many people carry into their old age a desperate yearning to be someone or do something that is no longer feasible. Some try to superimpose their dreams upon younger generations. The aspiring football hero now a grandfather pushes his grandson into the world of football. How can people in later years help one another accept the past, healing wounds when necessary? As congregations become centers for intimacy and renewal, elderly members may find courage to surrender outdated dreams. Equally challenging for congregations is to discover ways to help members find new hope and mold fresh dreams.

For a thoughtful discussion on giving up dreams, invite older people to react to these lines from John Greenleaf Whittier's poem "Maud Muller":

Of all sad words of tongue or pen,
The saddest are these: "It might have been."

As mentioned in the opening chapter of this book, our ageist society too often glorifies youth. No wonder so many gray-haired people reach for the bottle of dye, believing that a blonde, brunette, or auburn crown of glory will reduce the consequences of accumulated years. Growing gray or bald, however, does not automatically assure acceptance of age. It reminds the world that it is okay to grow older. In Dylan Thomas' poem "Do Not Go Gentle into That Good Night," the speaker pleads, "Rage, rage against the dying of the light." Do we interpret this plea as rebellion against the body's diminishing ability to function or as a rallying cry to live fully as long as we have breath? One hopes that people of faith, whether teenagers or centenarians, can wholeheartedly embrace their age even while recognizing their mortality.

Dealing with Death

Our Own Death

Just as we are engaged in caring for our living bodies, so also we need to be engaged in making plans regarding our death. Life insurance companies hound us with appeals for new policies. But financial arrangements are only one aspect of death preparation. Note the Engaging Example at the end of this chapter. It outlines a workable plan to help people get their affairs in order.

Our beliefs about eternal life help give shape to the ways we spend our days. Those who trust in God's goodness and mercy may view death as a welcome friend. If older adults are reluctant to discuss thoughts related to dying, however, they may still respond to topics such as preparing advance directives. Our sophisticated technological society has manufactured new dilemmas about extending life. We need guidance in sorting out alternatives.

One United Church of Christ located in Sun City, Arizona, has a well-equipped group called "Concerned Friends."[6] They assist church members and friends in anticipating, preparing for, and meeting some of the more serious problems related to advancing years. Concerned Friends has prepared a number of documents and study materials addressing the following issues:

- living will and health care power of attorney
- general durable power of attorney
- comparison of retirement options
- comparison of mortuaries
- church policy for use of memorial garden
- billfold emergency information card

Do you remember the childhood prayer "Now I lay me down to sleep"? That phrase "If I should die before I wake" takes on new meaning for people in later years. People flock to workshops titled simply "If I should die before . . . " Such occasions enable participants to ponder faith statements embodied in hymns and scripture that they want incorporated in their memorial service. Sharing their preferences with others, including clergy, aids them in clarifying theological beliefs.

Does your church have a columbarium, a designated site to receive the ashes of loved ones? Throughout history it has been the function of the church to baptize us when we are born and bury us when we die. In antiquity, cemeteries were always situated adjacent to the church. As churches abandoned their role of providing burial places, commercial cemeteries began assuming this responsibility. Now as churches develop columbaria, they proclaim the sacredness of life and help members accept death as a holy mystery.

Death of Others

In what ways can congregations respond at times of dying and death? Mortuaries and other secular institutions may offer instruction and support, but faith communities need to enfold grieving members with a sense of God's loving presence. In which of these suggestions does your church engage?

- Caring committee—an organized group that offers to provide meals, run errands, be in the home of the bereaved to answer the phone and help with other matters.

• Reception following memorial service—a time of gathering that gives the family an opportunity to interact with friends, to share memories, and to receive strength for continuing life.

• Memorial gifts—families may designate selected projects within the church, such as youth scholarships for work camps or planting a tree as part of property beautification. Beneficiaries of memorial gifts could also be altruistic funds, especially if they represent particular interests of the one who died. When older people see that the church has not forgotten their peers who die, they take heart in knowing that their own lives will also be remembered.

• Grief support groups—"I don't know what to do with my grief," moaned one widower. By bringing together people who have suffered the loss of a loved one, churches and synagogues can promote healing. In addition, caring individuals can informally invite one or two grieving people to eat together or share some other common experience. Creative listening is at the heart of helping people move through traumatic times.

• Anniversary acknowledgments—People in grief often dread the anniversaries of their loved one's birth, death, or marriage. Any significant reminder of shared memories can be painful. Have a person or group within the church contact the bereaved one on the anniversary date to express caring concern. In our church an older woman writes personalized notes to survivors one year after the death of the loved one. I have seen the remarkable response from recipients. The note writer also alerts church staff to the impending anniversary. Phone calls from clergy undergird the survivor's realization that he or she is not alone.

Anticipating death, the final universal event, leads us to reflect on the meaning of time, of our earthly days. With an accumulation of days and years, the elderly may acquire insights for living that help them deepen their faith in God and sustain them as they accept changes.

I find an enduring promise in the last paragraph of Kathleen Fischer's book *Winter Grace.*

Not only do older people find in their present experiences of dying and rising reasons to hope for the reality of life after death. They offer hope to us all. For in the paradoxes of their lives—strength in the midst of frailty, perseverance in the midst of brokenness, love despite pain and suffering, spiritual ascent transcending physical decline, faith and life-engagement at the edge of death—they witness to that miracle of new life which is at the heart of the Christian faith. Older people are winter grace not just for themselves and for each other, but for all of us.[7]

Engaging Examples

Are Your Affairs in Order?

St. Andrew's Presbyterian Church in Tucson, Arizona, has developed a planning guide and resource book titled *Are Your Affairs in Order?* Individuals may read it privately, or the booklet may be the basis for study and discussion sessions. The introduction reminds readers that "few of us take time to do the praying, thinking, talking and acting needed to prepare for the future. . . . Planning ahead is more than being practical; it is an act of love."

The book is divided into four categories:

- Personal and financial information (Includes worksheets for family data, names of consultants, location of important documents, plus a listing of assets and debts.)

- Spiritual planning and resources (Too often omitted from other check-lists. In addition to listing suggested passages of scripture and hymns to use for religious service, this section addresses numerous practical concerns such as preparing an obituary, determining disposition of body, and locating resources for coping with grief.)

- Health insurance and living arrangements (Includes a concise ex-planation of Medicare. Also gives guidelines for selecting nursing care, home health care, and hospice care.)

• Explanation of pertinent legal documents (Useful overview of advance directives, health care power of attorney, living will, probate issues, and organ and tissue donation.)

Some materials in this book have been adapted from material prepared by Dr. William Auld, 620 Plymouth Rd. #5, Claremont, CA, 91977, and Bryn Mawr Presbyterian Church, Bryn Mawr, PA. Although portions of this booklet are specific to St. Andrew's Church and the state of Arizona, it is a good example of what other congregations could develop.

Contact: Beverly J. Greer
St. Andrew's Presbyterian Church
750 West Chapala Drive
Tucson, AZ 85704
(520) 297-7201

Trinity Braille Ministry

Every week in Phoenix, Arizona, a group of about fifteen women gather at Trinity United Methodist Church to pursue a unique ministry. They produce braille copies of United Methodist church school literature, and study books, choir music, and worship bulletins for blind people at Trinity and other United Methodist churches throughout the United States. Four of the women are trained braillists with one additionally trained in music braille. The other volunteers are reproducing copies, typing, binding, and packing materials for mailing to various states. After being used by children or adults, the braille copies are sent overseas for use at mission schools for the blind.

Beth Appleby, a member of Trinity Church, started this program in 1982 because one of her piano students, also a singer in her children's choir, was blind. Appleby enrolled in an intensive course of study that trained her to be a braillist. The Library of Congress has certified her not only as a literary braillist but also as a music braillist. More women at Trinity Church, including the grandmother of the blind child, became certified for preparing braille materials. Most of these volunteers are older women who are deeply committed to this unique ministry. Bonds of affection and concern develop as the women work together week after week.

This project, started rather simply in one congregation of eight hundred members, now reaches around the world in providing braille copies of church-related resources for men, women, and children. The church also serves as a consulting center that helps connect volunteer braillists whom Appleby has recruited from all over the nation.

Guidelines from the Braille Ministry include reminders of how to help all people who are visually impaired. Braille labels on doors and walls assist braille users in knowing the location of various activities. A guidesheet includes useful suggestions:

• Encourage and enable blind and visually impaired people to take part in any and all aspects of church life, as participants and in leadership roles. If possible, involve these people in the decisions concerning special ministries.

• Make sure that sidewalks, hallways, and all passages are free from obstacles at ground level and above. This includes hanging branches, signs, light fixtures, furniture, and garbage cans.

• Offer to arrange transportation to and from church and a guide (if the person wants one) while at church events.

• Follow mailed announcements of church meetings with telephone calls or personal messages to blind and visually impaired people.

As members of this church have invested themselves on behalf of those unable to see, they have also become more aware of people with other disabilities. The resulting Committee on Ministries with the Disabled now provides a signer for worship services and other public meetings, has made sure that all rooms are wheelchair-accessible, has provided large-print copies of major publications, and made other hospitable accommodations. The committee coordinates a medical loan closet with wheelchairs, walkers, and other equipment available for members to use.

Although some older people may choose not to utilize signers or braille resources, they can become strong advocates on behalf of others needing special assistance. Beth Appleby, now retired from her music career, communicates passionately about her ministry. Her evangelistic fervor brings help and hope to people of all ages who are dealing with losses.

Contact: Trinity Braille Ministry
Beth Appleby
3104 W. Glendale Ave.
Phoenix, AZ 85051
(602) 973-1415

Points to Ponder

1. All of us change as we age. What changes have you noticed in your own physical body, psychic energy, spiritual awareness?

2. Gather your own "symbols of selfhood." Individually or in a small group reflect on what these symbols meant to you ten years ago. What do you think they will mean to you ten years into the future? If possible, share your thoughts in a small group.

3. Review your accumulation of personal possessions. Which kinds of things cause most clutter and frustration for you? Which items are precious treasures that you would be most reluctant to relinquish? What thoughts and plans do you have about passing your treasures on to others?

4. Which of your five senses do you think is most essential for living fully? Why? Many people of faith with physical limitations still enjoy meaningful lives. Share examples of such people who inspire you.

5. Letting go of dreams can be a crushing or liberating experience. Cite examples from your own life or lives of friends. In what ways was the church able or unable to provide consolation and hope?

6. Discuss the theological implications of the familiar phrase "I can do it by myself."

7. How is your congregation organized for ministry to people who have experienced the loss of a loved one?

CHAPTER 7

Living Longer, Stronger Lives

Health for Years—and More Years

Whenever I ask audiences how long they would like to live, their answers invariably reflect the same message: "I don't care how many years I'm around, just so long as I stay healthy and keep my mind." Frailty and dementia seem to be almost universal fears. Marketeers bombard aging consumers with promises that their cereal, facial cream, or vitamin supplements will enable users to remain forever young.

Research studies show that people remain active longer and die at an older age than was true a few decades ago. Living for one hundred years no longer astounds society. Many greeting card companies design products for people who are celebrating their one hundredth birthday. Books such as *Having Our Say: The Delany Sisters' First 100 Years* captivate readers.[1] Lynn Peters Adler devoted ten years to interviewing people who had lived for ten decades. As a result she wrote *Centenarians: The Bonus Years*.[2] Rich in human interest stories, her book also gives serious attention to the legacy of values and beliefs including spiritual dimensions. Based on her many interviews, Adler notes that religion and spirituality are central to most centenarians' lives. In her chapter dealing with the courage to grow old, the author makes the following observation.

> Centenarians say that a positive attitude combining hope, faith, love and optimism develops in earlier years and is then available to serve one well later on. This positive attitude and the ability to adapt are crucial in helping to combat the very real losses of aging and the life changes that occur as we grow older.[3]

Why do some people live so much longer than others? There is no simple answer to this question, but genetics probably contributes more than any other single factor to predicting the length of our lives. Advances in health care also have an impact on longevity. These include, for example, dramatic surgery such as organ transplantation and sophisticated cardiovascular interventions. Basic self care, however, is one area over which we have the most control as we age. As we will see, the lifestyles we choose make a marked difference in what happens to us physically, emotionally, and spiritually. Faith communities also have much to contribute to the area of self care.

Judeo-Christian Expressions of Wholeness and Healing

Although wholistic health care may appear on the surface to be a contemporary concept, its roots extend back to early Judaism. The shema, that basic commandment in Deuteronomy 6:4-9, declares that God is one. Believers are to love God with their whole heart, soul, and might. That all-encompassing love nourishes wellness. Passages in the Psalms celebrate God's power to heal all our diseases. The New Testament emphasizes Jesus' intention to heal the whole person. Nearly one-fifth of the material in the Gospels deals with stories of Jesus' healings. Wholeness of life is consistent with Jesus' message of good news. Jesus commissioned his disciples to preach the kingdom of God and to heal the sick.

Centuries passed; Christianity spread far beyond the Mediterranean basin. Religious orders established places to care for the sick and dying, particularly sojourners making pilgrimages to holy sites. Hospices offered a resting place for those travelers. Unfortunately, there were periods when the Church condemned medicine, creating a science versus faith rift that to some extent still exists today.

With the rise of the modern hospital movement, religious organizations often led the way in creating centers to care for the sick. Denominations founded homes for the aging as well as children's homes. But that care reached only a limited population. Now churches and synagogues are supporting ministries that help people of all ages remain as healthy as possible. The best example of this trend is the parish nurse movement.

Parish Nurse Ministry

Granger Westberg, a Lutheran pastor-professor, deserves primary credit for developing what has become the parish nurse movement. Early in the 1960s while serving a church in Springfield, Ohio, he started a wholistic health center. By the next decade, he was in the Chicago area working with a physician establishing a similar center. In cooperation with the University of Illinois College of Medicine and Lutheran General Health System, they began wellness clinics in churches.

Although many physicians recognize the importance of spiritual dimensions in promoting wellness, Westberg and his associates realized that nurses more often exhibit deep understanding of the need to combine faith and health promotion. Nurses who view life from a religious perspective want to work with the whole person. Serving as either a volunteer or paid staff member in a congregation, the parish nurse usually functions in the following roles:

- personal health counselor
- health educator
- community resource liaison
- organizer and coordinator of health concerns in congregation
- interpreter of relationship between faith and health

The nurse carries out all of these tasks—including visitation in homes, hospitals, and nursing homes—in partnership with clergy staff. Some congregations establish health committees or some other form of wellness committee. Volunteers, many of whom may be retired medical personnel, can help organize and promote such activities as blood pressure screening, flu shot clinics, lending closets with medical equipment, and visits to isolated people. An Engaging Example for this chapter features a parish nursing project in Iowa.

Older adults benefit from this whole-person minstry both as providers and as recipients of care. As parish nurses equip volunteers to be sensitive listeners, these recruits, whether young or old, can bring fresh hope and healing to aging members of churches and synagogues.

Latter Lifestyles

Focus on Self Care

As aging people live longer, stronger lives, stereotypes of tottering old
men and women start to melt. Instead, new images are emerging of
active retirees living the kind of abundant life that Jesus offers. Many
authors, including nursing professor Karen Johnson Kerner, are celebrating the healthy trend toward responsible self care.

> The negative illness model of aging—that one goes downhill
> steadily with age—is being replaced with the more positive well-
> ness model of aging. The wellness model proposes that one can
> achieve wellness throughout life, despite the presence of chronic
> conditions and other problems which are prevalent in later life . . . .
> The wellness model involves taking responsibility for one's own
> health and keeping the faith and hope which strengthens the ability
> to cope with life's changes.[4]

When the Governor of Arizona appointed me as a delegate to the
White House Conference on Aging held in May 1995, I hoped to pass
resolutions addressing spiritual needs of older Americans. Colleagues
and I who are active in religious gerontology strategized to assure that
resulting actions would reflect our priorities. Explicit reference to some
of our concerns did appear in the resolution titled "Encouraging development and ensuring implementation of advance directives, such as
living wills." Certainly we must give attention to such concerns related
to end-of-life issues, as discussed in the previous chapter. Our responsibilities within churches and synagogues, however, include encouraging
members to know and practice healthy lifestyles.

As had been predicted, the White House Conference resolutions
garnering the highest number of votes concerned keeping Social Security sound, preserving the integrity of the Older Americans Act, and issues
related to Medicaid and Medicare. As we seek to assure abundant life
for all in later years, we need to be informed about legislative developments concerning economic and health care matters. But we cannot rely
solely on government to keep people healthy.

Several resolutions at the 1995 conference pertained to self care, especially one labeled "Assuming personal responsibility for the state of one's health." As you read the following excerpts from that resolution, envision ways that churches and synagogues can make the intent become reality.

Whereas individuals make choices about food that they eat, the physical activity/ exercise in which they engage, and the lifestyle they lead;

Whereas many health problems can be prevented or alleviated by changes in behavior, lifestyle, or treatment plan . . .

Whereas older adults are normally their own primary providers of health care;

Therefore, be it resolved by the 1995 White House Conference on Aging to support policies that:

Ensure that all individuals, especially older adults and care givers, have full access to wellness and health educational programs, services and facilities, so that they may provide sufficient self-care and know when to seek appropriate professional care . . .

Educate all persons in the community about the diversity of the aging process, including possible physical, emotional, and social changes affecting older adults, and evaluate the effectiveness of such educational programs.[5]

Other sections of this resolution stress the need to promote self care among diverse cultural, racial, and linguistic groups, whether living in urban or rural settings. Implementing these resolutions will be a challenge to faith communities as we enter the twenty-first century.

As reported in the book *Religion, Health, and Aging*, researchers are giving increasing attention to the effect of religious beliefs, rituals, and experiences on our aging population.[6] When reviewing statistics about religious phenomena influencing mental and physical health of older people, I realized that results may sometimes be contradictory.

There seems to be ample evidence, however, that religion does make a difference. Implications from current research underscore the value of health care professionals and religious professionals working together. Guidance from a group of peer believers may be as important as support from professional leaders.

What are some specific ways religious beliefs affect health?

> Religious groups often promote a social environment that is conducive to healthy lifestyles. Smoking, excessive alcohol consumption, and illicit drug use are usually discouraged, and such behaviors may be viewed as contrary to doctrinal teachings. The lower frequency of adverse health behaviors among religiously active persons has been demonstrated in numerous epidemiologic surveys. . . . Support from church members may play a significant role in both instituting and maintaining lifestyle changes such as smoking cessation, discontinuation and moderation in drinking habits, and appetite control. Another study has shown that women who were active church members were more likely to participate in cervical cancer screening, indicating a greater concern over health maintenance.[7]

Health-promoting Habits

Each topic discussed below has an impact on the health of individuals. Although we usually view health as a private matter, ways we care for ourselves affect others around us. Sometimes it is easier to develop good health habits when supported by a group. What better group than members of a church or synagogue?

• Exercise
Swimming, walking, aerobic exercises—all these forms of physical activity help keep our bodies functioning as fully as possible. Help members within congregations to find exercise partners. This could include sign-up sheets for sports such as golf or tennis, bowling or hiking. Some churches offer weekly exercise sessions. Variations of jazzercise groups call themselves "praise-er-cize."

• Nutrition

The saying "you are what you eat" may be an overstatement, but its underlying truth makes sense. Did you ever consider how much time of your life you spend eating? This should be a pleasurable activity. But aging can present barriers to eating habits:

• Tooth and gum problems increase with age, so dental visits are important.
• Taste buds often shrink with age, resulting in diminished ability to distinguish tastes.
• Sense of smell deteriorates and affects flavor sensations.
• People living alone may no longer prepare nutritionally adequate meals.

Shared meals for retired people are probably one of the most common experiences provided through churches. These may be potluck, catered, or outings to restaurants. What a great way to foster fellowship. Programs about balanced diets, weight control, and good nutrition rank high with seniors. Nutrition-conscious church members may challenge the cookie or donut routine too prevalent at refreshment time. Fruits and vegetables or other healthy snacks may replace calorie-laden sweets.

• Freedom from harmful chemicals

You can probably list the pollutants to your body that daily jeopardize good health: tobacco, alcohol, excess salt, drugs negatively interacting with other drugs. Twelve-step programs, such as Alcoholics Anonymous, illustrate again the power of support groups for establishing healthy habits. Does your church prohibit smoking? Are skilled staff available to counsel people about alcoholism or refer them to community agencies? To ignore such issues suggests that we do not care about what happens to people's bodies, minds, and spirits.

• Adequate sleep

As essential for the body as food and water is sleep. Sleep patterns may change as we grow older, but major problems are not an inevitable part of aging. Older adults are usually eager for information from physicians specializing in sleep disorders. Congregations who make use of such expertise learn the importance of establishing a regular schedule for going to sleep and getting up. Groups of older people may share ideas about how to create a safe and comfortable environment for sleeping as well as personal approaches for inducing sleep. Life can be more meaningful when the body is rested.

• Safety awareness
According to the U.S. Department of Health and Human Services, every year 650,000 people over the age of sixty-five are injured by accidents in the home. Most of these accidents are preventable. Many injuries result from hazards that can be eliminated. Safety education conducted through churches and synagogues may reduce falls and other causes of unnecessary suffering.

One of the most innovative programs I know in this field is Project Safe Home. The Volunteer Interfaith Caregivers Program of Phoenix in partnership with a major utility company, the Salt River Project, developed a safety inspection and repair program.[8] Trained volunteers conduct the inspection using a home injury prevention checklist. Volunteers make minor repairs or alterations such as installing grab bars, smoke alarms, peepholes in doors, and making rugs skid-proof. Designed to aid disabled and homebound older adults, this program is one you can readily adapt to various settings.

Health-affirming Therapies

Many approaches in the health care field that are labeled as therapies can also be used for preventive purposes. Let your imagination suggest ways that the following so-called therapies can be integrated into the lives of congregations.

• Pet therapy
Pet lovers find great satisfaction sharing with others the stories about their cats, dogs, or other treasured creatures. Some people in later years may have difficulty caring for animals. This may be a natural place for church members young and old to interact.

• Gardening therapy
Digging in the "good earth" can bring physical, emotional, and spiritual

rewards. Again, this can be a natural transgenerational activity. What a great way to bring people together—to share food and flowers. Bodies stiff with arthritis may still be able to cultivate plants in special flower or vegetable boxes raised to an appropriate height.

• Bibliotherapy
Worlds of adventure, learning, and inspiration await us through printed or recorded words. Reading sometimes becomes more pleasurable when we discuss reactions with others. Script-in-hand reading of plays lets readers become characters. For those with visual impairment, large-print books and magazines are a bonanza. Most public libraries can provide literature on audiotape.

• Play therapy
Having fun boosts our bodies, minds, and hearts. If we think we are too old to be silly, then we *are* too old! Images linger of religion as puritanical, strait-laced, and opposed to having fun. But current research, including highly popularized writings by the late Norman Cousins, underscores the necessity for humor in our lives. Some congregations have cartoon boards; others include jokes in newsletters. Being able to put life in perspective can replace heavy-hearted attitudes with light-hearted spirits.

Health Care for All

If our focus is exclusively on promoting wellness for ourselves, we betray our Judeo-Christian teachings. Primary commandments tell us to love our neighbors as ourselves. Wholeness for everybody is a matter of faith and justice. This is where creative advocacy comes to the foreground.

In 1993 three United Church of Christ congregations in the greater Lansing, Michigan, area published a curriculum designed to help churches address issues related to health care reform.[9] The course begins with a stirring quotation from Dr. Martin Luther King, Jr.: "Of all forms of inequality, injustice in health is the most shocking and inhuman."

In some respects, this study program focuses on the health care crisis of the 1990s. Following six chapters packed with information and user-friendly resources, however, the curriculum concludes with practical suggestions to help learners become skillful advocates. Included are down-to-earth tips on how to organize letter-writing campaigns. The authors offer additional guidelines for effective political action.

Even if retirees do not become involved in direct contact with legislators, they can seek out ways to improve living conditions in their own communities. This may be as basic as visiting and perhaps volunteering in food banks, supporting shelters for the homeless, and investigating health care provisions for low income families. Seniors groups having meals together may request those attending to bring nonperishable food items to donate to designated charities. In one church the donated food becomes table decorations for monthly luncheons.

Longer, stronger lives are not just for privileged populations. Access to health and wholeness is a basic human right that should be available to God's children—all ages!

Engaging Examples

TempleCare

When I first learned about this program, I noted with interest the red-letter invitation printed at the bottom of a promotional sheet. "You are cordially invited to join us for intriguing discussions on your physical, mental, and spiritual 'Temple.'" What a fresh way to lift up the passage from 1 Corinthians 3:16, "Do you not know that you are God's temple and that God's Spirit dwells in you?"

TempleCare presentations and discussions are part of the ministry with older adults organized through a committee at Walnut Street Baptist Church in Louisville, Kentucky. On the third Thursday of each month seniors attend TempleCare. If they wish, they may purchase a nominally priced lunch. Featured topics offered during one year include:

"Everyday Miracles in Medicine"
"Striving toward a Healthy Heart"
"Skin—A Good Cover-up"
"The Aging Eye"
"Open Wide—Dental Health for Adults"

"So You're Facing Surgery"
"Long-Term Health Care Insurance"

Started in 1990, this series continues attracting people from inner-city Louisville as well as those from the more affluent suburban sections. No matter where people live, they are all responsible for their bodies, their temples. Many of the speakers at TempleCare meetings are members of the sponsoring church; other presenters come from health organizations. According to the current director, Gene Sutherland, some of the most profound speakers are faculty members at Louisville universities, medical school, and community colleges. Most speakers are willing to come for a modest honorarium or no fee. To be most effective, Sutherland suggests that those attending TempleCare actually propose topics and secure speakers.

Contact: Gene Sutherland
Walnut Street Baptist Church Dining Room
220 W. St. Catherine Street
Louisville, KY 40203
(502) 589-5290

Parish Nursing in Iowa

Although the parish nurse movement began in the Chicago area, it has much to offer the congregations in small towns and rural areas. The community of Spencer, Iowa—population of 11,500—provides a helpful example of this type of ministry. A nurse from Sioux City, Iowa, heard Granger Westberg explain the benefits of a parish nurse ministry. That nurse inspired Jan Striepe, a community health nurse in Spencer, to explore this idea with her congregation, Trinity Lutheran Church in Spencer. Although Jan Striepe works full-time with the Northwest Iowa Aging Association, she found time to organize people in her church to develop this caring ministry.

As often happens, the church discovered that there were several retired nurses willing to volunteer time. Next, by writing a successful grant proposal, Jan Striepe secured modest funding for a part-time parish nurse. Now, ten years later, Trinity Lutheran Church in Spencer has two

paid nurses who each work four hours a week. In addition to being
skilled listeners, they can also refer parishioners to appropriate agencies.
Transportation to medical appointments in major metropolitan centers
can be a big problem; this problem can be even more difficult for rural
residents. Nurses may enlist and coordinate volunteer drivers. Other
functions of nonurban parish nurses, such as organizing annual health
fairs, offering CPR classes, and presenting wellness seminars, incorporate a wholistic philosophy. According to Ms. Striepe, another primary
function of the parish nurse is to engage in prayer with people seeking
help.

Contact: Jan Striepe, R.N.
1111 8th Ave. W.
Spencer, Iowa 51301
(712) 262-1775

For further information on parish nursing, contact The International
Parish Nurse Resource Center in Park Ridge, Illinois (see appendix A.)

Points to Ponder

1. In your congregation what basic hopes and fears do people have about
living long, long lives? How can you address those fears?

2. Which hospitals or medical centers in your region were founded by
religious organizations? Have these religious organizations continued
supporting the medical institutions? What differences do you perceive
between church and synagogue related non-profit health institutions and
for-profit health institutions?

3. Why are churches and synagogues appropriate places for fostering
wellness? What health promotion activities does or might your congregation offer? Evaluate your congregation's involvement in the following
categories:

• exercise
• nutrition

- freedom from chemical dependency
- safety awareness
- general health promotion

4. How can your church library relate to health and wellness needs of older people?

5. If we believe that "merry hearts are good medicine," then we need to create opportunities for experiencing joy and fun. How do you integrate humor into the life of your congregation?

6. Advocacy requires careful study and effective action. What local, state, or national issues related to inclusive health care could the older people in your congregation tackle? If your community has active advocacy groups, such as the League of Women Voters or the Older Women's League, confer with them about ways to be in partnership.

CHAPTER 8

Creating as Process and Product

What Is Creativity?

"In the beginning God created ..." That creative force surging through the universe—and through all time and space—finds expression in human beings. We are creators with God, able to put together our experiences in surprising ways. Creativity is not so much a product as a process, not so much an ability as an attitude. How can churches learn from and with older people the joys of expressing ideas and concerns in fresh ways? Responses to that question are the focus of this chapter.

Books on creativity crowd shelves in libraries and bookstores. One popular volume is *The Artist's Way: A Spiritual Path to Higher Creativity* by Julia Cameron with Mark Bryan.[1] The phrase "A Course in Discovering and Recovering Your Creative Self" appears on the cover. Early in the book the authors describe basic principles of creativity that they call "spiritual electricity." Their principles reflect the following truths: flowing through all of us is an underlying force we call creativity; in endowing everyone with this force, God invites us to grow and change. I believe that this spiritual electricity is available for people at any stage of their lives. Those who have lived many years may be apt interpreters of the spirit of spontaneity permeating creativity.

As we encourage elders to express their thoughts and feelings, their doubts and fears, they may do so verbally. There are countless other ways, however, in which we explore and reveal our personhood. If we honestly believe in a creator God who treasures our uniqueness, then our religious institutions need to develop ways for celebrating uniqueness. God's way is not a paint-by-number approach. Instead, God equips us with senses, skills, and spirits that can lead us into adventures of the soul.

Generativity as a Dimension of Creativity

In 1963 when Erik Erikson expounded in *Childhood and Society* his eight stages for human development, he championed for adults the importance of generativity as opposed to stagnation.[2] In essence, the concept of generativity suggests helping people move out of ruts into more satisfying behaviors. Sometimes we impose these ruts on ourselves; in other cases, circumstances including social conditions discourage people from exploring possibilities in their lives. Generativity of the spirit takes us beyond childbearing to include elements of spontaneity and imagination.

A chapter in *Aging and the Religious Dimension* stresses the relationship of creativity and generativity.[3] Generativity is, according to the authors, a need to outlive the self in spiritual terms. Having children is a natural way to attempt some sort of immortality. We see this played out in the nurturing roles of men and women. People born in the first third of the twentieth century experienced fairly stereotypical gender roles. Society expected women to concentrate on nurturing children, and men usually had the responsibilities of providing financial support. Those roles are less clear-cut today, yet many of our oldest generations still feel comfortable with the idea that the woman's place is in the home.

Although people of retirement age usually do not conceive and bear children, they can still give birth to ideas. Such ideas become the basis for new behaviors, for risking and trying different approaches, perhaps for altering ways of doing a routine task. This is not just a matter of "teaching old dogs new tricks." Rather, it is encouraging the old dog to make up the new tricks. A widow who found evening mealtime an especially lonely time decided to surround that dinner hour with favorite recorded music that she and her late husband had particularly enjoyed. Her simple act brought an inner satisfaction. One older man grew bored walking his dog the same way every morning. His decision to alter his route brought him into contact with others walking their dogs. Those contacts eventually led to new friendships. "I should have tried a new path long ago," he observed.

Imagination and Creativity

How long has it been since you watched young children at play? Electronic gadgetry and technological wonders can boggle the minds of
parents and almost overwhelm some grandparents. Toystores these days
appear to be warehouses of mechanical and technological wizardry. Yet
youngsters may still find fascination in creating ships and skyscrapers
out of discarded boxes. Even making tents out of old blankets draped
over dining room chairs opens doors to imaginative play.

What helps to unleash imaginative powers for older people? If men
or women in later years begin talking about "imaginary playmates" or
some equivalent of fictitious characters, we may surmise that dementia
is beginning. That very quality of pretending what is or might be, an
attribute cherished in children, we tend to scorn in adulthood.

Of course, we do talk about fantasies that can mask reality at any
age. Such longing for experiences beyond reach need not be abnormal.
The ancient prophet Joel declared, "Old men shall dream dreams" (Joel
2:28). Words of twentieth-century prophet Martin Luther King, "I have
a dream," continue to echo around the world.

What, then is the desirable role of imagination for older people?
How do churches and synagogues cultivate the use of imagination as a
tool for deepening faith? Certainly the fine arts—music, drama, painting, literature—and other forms of expression have conveyed theological insights over the centuries. Stained glass windows and medieval
passion plays became means of teaching biblical stories. Later in this
chapter we will discuss the role the liberal arts play in older people's
imaginations.

Many present-day retirees were Depression babies born in an era
of economic scarcity. People now in their seventies and eighties lived
through years when their families raised their own fruits and vegetables;
women sewed clothes for their families, often making over hand-me-
downs to fit the next youngest child. For some hardy souls, lack of material possessions encouraged a make-do attitude: If you did not have
money to buy elaborate or even simple furnishings for the home, you
made do with what was available. Orange crates could be simple book
cases. Creative touches turned crude objects into attractive examples of
ingenuity.

Aging relatives today may disparage the thought of young married

couples starting life in a fancy four bedroom house, two cars in the garage, and money for country club living. Their "when we were young"
litany is of little value unless it accompanies a willingness to imagine
what might be and then alter what is until it becomes what is imagined.

Elderly church members may respond in varying ways to memories
of their earlier years with limited incomes. For some, a pattern of fru-
gality continues. There may be a reluctance to spend and a tendency to
save, even hoard. On the other hand, those who resented deprivations in
childhood may vow to "eat, drink, and be merry," spending all they
have, even running up huge debts. Such contrasting attitudes can have a
serious impact on how members of congregations want to spend or save
the church's money. But if leaders can inspire others to dream—or
fantasize—about what might be, then creative energies may accomplish
remarkable things.

Creativity in Congregations

Within the life of churches we often find resistance to experimenting, to
trying new ways. When older people take the risk of doing something in
a new way, however, they may become the strongest proponents for
change. This has happened in churches that have altered times or styles
of worship. When one large metropolitan church decided to initiate a
Saturday evening worship hour, some of the most vocal advocates were
people in their seventies and eighties.

Ownership of creations may bring the creators a sense of worth. A
group of retirees in one congregation noticed that the entrance to their
educational building looked lifeless. After a series of lively planning
sessions, they designed a small garden with flowers blooming from
spring through autumn. They could say of their project with great pride,
"That's our baby!" Note that this very image of a baby reflects the
concept of generativity.

Life filled with the Spirit cannot be boring. St. Augustine's pro-
clamation, "A Christian should be an alleluia from head to foot," cap-
tures the sense of energy that can flow through congregations. Here are
a few examples of activities launched by older members that can inspire
congregations:

- using computers to create personalized greeting cards to send to homebound friends
- inviting children to a pumpkin-carving party
- decorating cookies for holiday teas
- developing a loan closet of medical equipment
- setting up a "help yourself" table where people can share their used magazines
- organizing visits to community agencies that offer significant services often needed by members of the congregation
- advocating for justice issues including local concerns such as school board elections

Holding a "CAN-DO" festival is an ambitious but gratifying experience. It involves asking people in the congregation to identify particular activities they can do and would be willing to help others do. On a designated date have participants display their wares or show their activities for others to see. Provide a table or space for each participant for his or her activity. Those attending the festival will circulate among the displays and see who likes to do what. Entries may include activities such as stone polishing, woodcarving, speaking Spanish, baking unusual breads, flower pressing, knitting and other needlework, and photography.

The next step is as important as setting up displays. This step involves having people sign up to learn from those who can do. The resulting mentoring can bring people together who otherwise might never interact. A woman who demonstrates "creative cooking for one" discovers that other singles also want to vary their meals. People who enjoy table games such as bridge, backgammon, or chess find partners for future game playing. Beginning quilters learn a traditional skill that they may later pass on to their children. There is no limit to the creative possibilities at CAN-DO festivals.

Ways to Encourage Creativity

In many ways creativity is a very personal experience. It involves a steady series of choices including such basic decisions as what to wear, what to eat, what to say, and how to allocate time and money. One doesn't typically learn how to be creative from a book or formal in-struction. There are, nevertheless, valuable insights in books about creativity.

Mary Baird Carlsen's book *Creative Aging: A Meaning-Making Perspective* includes rich observations about creativity.[4] As a psychologist and psychotherapist, Carlsen addresses needs of the whole person, including spiritual dimensions. Although her book may be most applicable for people working in the caring professions, her insights can be very enlightening for readers of varied backgrounds. Particularly useful for leaders in churches are her chapters titled "Pioneers in a New Prime of Life" and "Our Elders at the Conference Table." These appear in the section labeled "Learning from Our Elders."

Another and much less academic book is *The Ageless Spirit* by Connie Goldman and Phillip Berman. Composed of interviews with animated, spirited older people, the book may inspire readers to explore their own spirit of adventure. Eda LeShan's story is representative of what the authors uncovered in their interviews:

> Lobsters get real crowded inside their three-pound shell—they're terribly uncomfortable—and it's not possible for them to go on living if they stay in that shell. So they go out to the sea unprotected, which is dangerous—they might get hit by a reef, they might be eaten by another lobster or fish—they must deshell. That whole hard shell comes off and the pink membrane that's inside grows and becomes a harder shell, but a bigger one. . . . The thing that you need more than anything else when you get old is the courage of a lobster. You are going to go through things where you have to become more flexible.[5]

Helping individuals express themselves freely, without any "shell," requires a climate of trust and of encouragement. Faith communities are natural environments for liberating members to share their creative selves. This can happen in various ways. People who have been teachers may serve as resource coordinators for education ministries; those with experience and wisdom in community needs may help promote outreach projects; people skilled in interior design have expertise for decorating church school rooms. Some older adults, rather than wanting to work in areas where they have experience, now prefer to explore new areas of service.

As individuals exhibit a spirit of freedom to be inventive, then groups working together may also take risks. Older people can enliven a task force or committee. If they are invited only as a token gesture to "honor the white hairs," then their input may not be taken seriously. But if leaders open doors for fresh thinking, even modeling the style with no-holds-barred brainstorming, exciting results may emerge.

Well-designed seminars and conferences can also spark innovative thought. In 1996 the Baptist Senior Adult Ministries affiliated with the Washington, D.C., Baptist Convention held a two-day conference with the theme "Still Bearing Fruit." That phrase from Psalm 92:14 became the launching pad for a series of thought-provoking workshops. Notice how the fruit analogy permeated many workshop titles:

"Bearing Fruit through Spiritual Growth"
"Share Your Fruit: Volunteer!"
"Still Fruity after All These Years" (with a focus on humor)
"Bible Study: Fruit for All Seasons"
"Still Bearing Fruit: Grandparenting in Challenging Times"

Other workshops at this conference dealt with essential topics such as "Staying Safe in a World of Crime," "Dating, Marriage, and Re-marriage after Fifty," and "Filling the Hole in the Soul." Underlying every session was the assumption that senior adults talking and thinking together can increase their creative response to living.

Fostering the Arts

Not everyone aspires to be a Beethoven or a Shakespeare, yet that does not prevent individuals from appreciating works of other creative geniuses. As we discuss ways that older adult ministries can incorporate the arts, we will consider three approaches. The first involves appreciation, the second involves participation, and the third involves actual creation of some art form.

The church and the arts have been in partnership since the beginning of Christianity. Symbols on the walls in the catacombs, underground burial places dating back to the first century A.D., are evidence that believers used artful representation to communicate their faith.

Even before that we find repeated reference in the Hebrew Scriptures to such artistic forms of expression as music and dance. Today both younger and older adults can find satisfaction in studying biblical passages related to the arts. One church hosted neighboring churches for a series of study sessions titled "Ever Since King David." Woven through the series were ancient and contemporary examples of artistic expressions we associate with David: music, meditation, and dance. Under skillful leadership, participants became bold enough to try making up simple tunes, writing modern-day psalms, and choreographing natural movements for familiar hymns. Such learning opportunities lend themselves to combining all three elements of incorporating the arts into ministry with older adults: appreciation, participation, and creation.

Appreciation of the arts can happen on an individual basis or with groups. People unable to be physically active outside their homes can still be consumers of the arts. Resources abound in the form of books, other printed materials, radio and television programs, audiocassettes or compact disc recordings. Most homebound people look forward to visitors. Why not arrange for a few people to meet in a home where together they can enjoy a performance of classical music on television, for example? Videotapes providing vicarious excursions such as tours of world-famous cathedrals can also bring people together. Libraries are fertile sources for such informal programs.

As mentioned earlier, people of faith throughout the centuries have been responding to God's presence—or their search for God's presence—by composing music, painting murals, designing cathedrals, and fashioning sculptures. In the field of literature alone there has been a steady procession of poetry, novels, hymn texts, plays, opera librettos, and prayers. Such a list goes on and on. Exploring this rich heritage of the fine arts is a significant avenue for older adult ministries.

Many older groups like to take trips. Consider going together to attend concerts or plays. Movies such as "Mr. Holland's Opus" stimulate thinking and practically beg for discussion. Special tours of art museums or other cultural institutions enable people to interact and expand their fine-arts horizons.

Moving beyond the more passive consumption of the arts, we next consider how to help seniors participate directly in art-related experiences. Music offers numerous examples for participation. People as old as eighty or ninety may continue singing in church choirs. Voice range and breathing become somewhat limited, but the best way for people to keep their singing voices strong is to keep singing. For over twenty years I directed a choir of residents in a retirement campus. The average age was eighty-four. Sometimes residents would say wistfully, "I used to sing in a choir, but now my voice isn't any good." With encouragement they resumed singing and happily discovered that they can still "make a joyful noise to the Lord." Older people can also find enjoyment in playing hand bells or hand chimes.

Closely related to participation is creation. Obvious examples include writing poetry or composing music—in contrast to listening to poems being read or singing existing music. One of the most popular forms of expression for people in retirement years is painting and other forms of visual arts. Invite experienced artists within your church or community to teach courses on watercolors or acrylics. One mid-sized church developed a strong reputation for having painting classes for men. Most of these men were retired; several were recovering from serious strokes. Each class developed camaraderie; in addition to producing art, the students cultivated fellowship.

Benefits of Creative Expressions

Older adult ministries can help make visible and accessible the creative selves that God yearns for us to be. Releasing childlike enthusiasm by expressing thoughts and feelings—no matter what the medium—helps to heal bodies and minds. Creativity contributes to wholeness; it engages our minds, bodies, emotions, and spirits. As we trust the creative process we enter the realm of mystery and awe, reflections of God.

The Artist's Way concludes with this prayer:

> O Great Creator, we are gathered together in your name that we may be of greater service to you and to our fellows. We offer ourselves as instruments. We open ourselves to your creativity in our lives. We surrender to you our old ideas. We trust that you will lead us. . . . Help us to know we are not alone, that we are loved and lovable. Help us to create as an act of worship to you.[6]

Engaging Examples

Arts and Older Adults Project

Presbyterian minister Dr. William E. Guilford has focused his ministry in the area of spirituality and creativity. In 1965, shortly after graduating from seminary, Dr. Guilford went to Oklahoma City. There he joined the staff of KOCO, one of the city's television stations, as producer of educational and religious programming. Then, from 1971 to 1984, he directed the Media and the Arts Agency, which involved eighteen different denominations in Oklahoma. This agency sponsored religion and arts festivals and produced television programs featuring arts in worship.

Bill Guilford often comments that art enhances life from beginning to end. For the past decade Bill has applied that philosophy to older people. Through workshops, conferences, and retreats he seeks to help older members of churches and synagogues find meaning and significance in their lives. He incorporated many of his ideas when he was part-time Associate Minister to Older Adults at First Presbyterian Church, Norman, Oklahoma.

Bill Guilford broadened his impact significantly when he became Coordinator for the Arts and Older Adults Project, Senior Adult Services, College of Continuing Education at the University of Oklahoma. Some of his projects can be adapted to local congregations.

- Workshops—whether intergenerational or limited to the senior population—explore dance, storytelling, printmaking, sculpture, clowning, pottery, and other disciplines.
- Community festivals and fairs feature talented older adults in areas of music, dance, fine arts, and drama.
- The Older Adults Traveling Arts Exhibit sets an example that congregations, either individually or collectively, could follow by developing exhibits to share with the wider community.
- Workshops in "readers theatre" have helped older adults improve public speaking skills.Participants read scenes from plays, monologues, stories, poetry, scripture, litanies, prayers, and other literary forms. Then they perform in worship, at other gatherings in their churches, and at retirement facilities or community centers.

In a letter to me, Bill expressed his enthusiasm for integrating the arts in older adult ministries.

> As people grow older, they often find that art, both its execution and appreciation, becomes a meaningful experience, sometimes in ways not found when they were younger or in the busy world of making a living and rearing a family. And they find that experiencing art enhances their spiritual growth, adding to or reinforcing their understanding of the meaning of life and its possibilities.
>
> The aging population can find outlets for art experience in cooperation with younger people, often under the aegis of the church and its functions. Churches become institutions where an intergenerational approach to aesthetic nourishment can be explored and executed, with benefit to both old and young.

Contact: Dr. William E. Guilford
9601 Hefner Village Blvd.
Oklahoma City, OK 73162
(405) 728-0968

SoulCare

Dorothie Wright's career as a director of religious education together with her talent in the visual arts equips her to combine effectively key elements of spirituality and creativity. She exemplifies men and women in every community who have developed their artistic skills and may be seeking opportunities to encourage others in creative adventures. Working through congregations and retreat centers, Dorothie, in collaboration with other SoulCare presenters, offers several special programs.

• Positive Eldering—Through music, art, poetry, and stories, this workshop explores the difference between aging and eldering.

• Morning Watch—In response to an elder story, such as Grimm's "Bremen Town Musicians," participants in the ongoing program relate the tale to their personal stories. As stories emerge, the leader encourages members of the group to write them out as fairy tales or poetry. These can be shared within congregations through newsletters or as separate collections of stories. Often the resulting wisdom becomes a basis for theological reflection.

- Art and Soul Workshop—This workshop, done in retirement facilities and senior centers as well as in churches, focuses on the experience of working with clay. The very process of molding the clay becomes symbolic of ways in which we shape our lives. As each person works with the clay, there is silence, music, and readings. At the close of the session, every participant has an opportunity to share reactions to the experience of working with clay. They may also create written expressions of their experience. Dorothie Wright remarks, "It's amazing what emerges from the hands and souls of supposed nonartists."

Contact: Dorothie Wright
10 Shoalwater Rd.
North Scituate, MA 02066
(617) 545-9069

Points to Ponder

1. In what ways do you express God's creative energy in your life?

2. Have you ever experienced periods of stagnation? What situation or conditions may have put you in a rut? How did you get out of the rut? Were there elements of faith that helped to liberate you?

3. People in later years are becoming more conscious of gender issues. Invite retirees to share ideas about how roles for men and women are changing. What are the implications of these changes for creativity?

4. Encourage older people to tell stories of their tactics for surviving tough times. How have their religious beliefs contributed to sustaining them through periods of economic, physical, or emotional crisis?

5. Analyze in your congregation the presence of aging people as leaders. How are their contributions productive or counterproductive? In what ways might their talents and wisdom be used more fully?

6. Cite examples of older people you know who are flexible and have the "courage of a lobster" (see quotation from *The Ageless Spirit*).

7. In which dimension of the arts is your congregation most involved: appreciation, participation, or creation? Observe which of these approaches attracts the most older people.

8. What opportunities exist in your community for older adults to create? How might congregations and community organizations work more closely together to foster creativity?

CHAPTER 9

Harvesting Faith Stories— Spiritual Eldering

The Value of Sharing Life Stories

Experiences from each human life could fill chapters and chapters. Although some people plead that their years have been boring and without drama, every man and woman is a walking book. A challenge for congregations is to help older members recognize the unique and precious qualities of their stories. Not only are such stories gold mines of memories, they also often highlight basic themes that permeate lives. Moreover, they become a means of transferring values and faith experiences from one generation to another.

How can congregations best enable older people to share life stories in ways that deepen their awareness of their own spiritual dimensions and also bring more meaning to their days? This chapter will explore the values inherent in sharing life stories and ways that churches can develop programs to help older people review their faith journeys.

Values for the Individual

"Who am I?" is a basic question that begs for response throughout our lives. A major task for older people, indeed for people of any age, is to review experiences and search for themes that integrate life. Our existence is meant to be more that just a collection of events and responses. Which events have been most instrumental in shaping our lives? When we look back over the years, what insights do we gain regarding our relationship to God as well as to family and all with whom we interact?

Erik Erikson, writing about developmental tasks of later years, cites the importance of combating tendencies toward despair with approaches that foster a sense of integrity.[1] In 1963 Dr. Robert Butler, then director of the National Institute on Aging, wrote a significant article titled "The Life Review: An Interpretation of Reminiscence in the Aged."[2] His article launched a major movement encouraging older people to reflect on their lives and share their thoughts and feelings with others.

As people explore the fabric of their days, they may experience numerous benefits:

- an increased awareness of dominant themes shaping their lives
- a sense of their own importance as a child of God
- a need for reconciling unfinished business from the past
- an appreciation of contributions from family and friends in developing their lives
- fresh insights into directions for the future
- new exploration of ways that God's presence has or has not been acknowledged
- a clarification of ideas about what is of lasting meaning in their lives

Values for Family and Friends

"Who are you?" That question, addressed to someone who has lived sixty or seventy or more years, can produce remarkable results. Layers of living may cover up rich stories waiting to be discovered. The dialogue approach of Jewish philosopher Martin Buber, with his emphasis on an I-Thou relationship, applies well to the role of interviewer and interviewee. As younger generations reach out to those in retirement years, a deep respect and affection may develop. Such bonds can lead to abiding ties that nourish the spirits of all involved.

When older people start recalling "the good old days" or the "dreadful old days," it may be tempting for family and friends to dismiss such talk. When we admonish people with a "don't-live-in-the-past" retort, we are rejecting the unique experience of the speaker. Instead, we need to encourage narrators to share freely those memories that live on in their souls. Some of these may open wounds not fully healed. Careful listening without judging can assist the speaker to gain confidence in dealing with haunting memories, ones that might be destructive rather than constructive.

Intentional sharing of stories can enable the listener, whether it be a relative or caring friend, to understand behavior and attitudes. A man or woman who has exhibited ongoing fear of thunderstorms, for example, may be able to recall childhoood situations in which storms produced anxiety. Perhaps there had been no one to reassure a child during crashing sounds and flashing sights. Decades later, such unresolved fears may be confronted in the course of reminiscing. With the help of sensitive listeners, the fearful one may discover ways to deal with this specific problem. Moreover, those who are listening may suddenly realize why the speaker has for years been unable to deal maturely with thunderstorms. Both speaker and listener can then move forward with new understandings.

Families often beseech older members to tell stories of their younger years. In fact, many publishing companies are producing books designed for grandparents or other later generations to fill in the blanks. Titles such as *Grandma Was Quite a Girl* are popular as guides suggesting categories for creative reminiscing.[3] Common topics include memories of school days, pets, life work, and family traditions connected with holidays.

Several sources are available for encouraging such general recall. For over twenty years two women in Madison, Wisconsin, have been developing Bi-Folkal Productions. Their creative materials include slides, photos, and large-print discussion starters.[4] Even though they market their products largely to senior centers and retirement communities, their materials can be useful for fellowship groups in congregations. Also, the American Association of Retired Persons distributes a booklet titled "Creative Reminiscing."

Although such resources are important, they may stop short of considering critical values that shape lives. Congregations can become involved in finding ways to be even more reflective.

Values for Congregations

Who are we as a family of faith? Not only does each person bring a faith story, but each church or synagogue also has its own life story.

Historians for any organization play a significant role in recording challenges faced, decisions made, and dreams achieved or deferred. Often it is the older members in a religious community who hold cherished memories of former years. As they pass on tales of struggles as well as triumphs, they enrich the understanding of younger generations. Every institution needs chroniclers who can interpret as well as record. Learning from the past is essential for each church or synagogue. Although there is no guarantee that older people automatically bring wisdom to situations, there is a strong likelihood that with creative interaction on the part of all ages, the insights gained from reviewing the past can shed light on the coming years.

In more theological arenas, older people may embody biblical truths. As people of the Word, we do well to identify with those who have wrestled many decades with the Word. Senior citizens still active in churches do not necessarily have an edge on younger people in figuring out what the universe is all about. Accounts of their own faith journeys, however, can inspire younger, less seasoned travelers to take heart and persevere in their own pilgrimage.

Approaches for Eliciting Faith Stories

Individuals Working Alone

Self-instruction is a common form of learning for old and young. Some folks need very little encouragement to record their faith stories. Many retired people regularly keep a diary or journal. Outstanding examples of people whose works are useful models include May Sarton, Florida Scott-Maxwell, and Elizabeth Vining. Excerpts from the writings of these three women all appear in Harry Berman's book *Interpreting the Aging Self: Personal Journals in Later Life.*[5]

Individuals Working with a Tutor or Class

Although individuals can read books to get ideas about writing their own autobiographies, such information is often best introduced in a group setting. Many community colleges as well as senior centers offer courses about writing one's life story. Written for such a purpose is *Guiding Autobiography Groups for Older Adults* by James Birren and Donna Deutchman.[6] While the emphasis in their book is on helping individuals gain a deepened awareness and appreciation of self, interaction with others is also emphasized. One chapter outlines eleven specific themes to use in developing life stories. Each theme begins with an overview of major branching points in each person's history. Specific subjects encompass family life, career, financial issues, health, death, love, and the arts. The final assignment deals with stress. Fortunately, those with experience guiding writing groups can advise less experienced leaders.

> The topics chosen for personal exploration and group interaction in guided autobiography are designed to focus attention and stimulate recall of memories of the formative experiences of life that are emotionally salient. By directing attention to the emotional issues and events of life, the group leader guides participants in the search for self-understanding. The leader provides a context in which exploration and, in a sense, the retelling and reliving of important experiences open the door to greater understanding and possibly even acceptance of one's past and current feelings.[7]

Journaling Retreats

Keeping a journal provides another opportunity for people of all ages to reflect in writing about who they are. Over the last dozen years, I have facilitated half-day, full-day, and even weekend retreats the sole purpose of which is to allow people to experiment with various ways of journal writing. Such events includes the following approaches:

Introduction to Creating Metaphors

A journaling retreat becomes more focused if it is designed around a common theme. That theme also becomes a point of departure for introducing specific kinds of writing. If the theme is "Weaving the Threads," then ask people to tell how they compare themselves to a kind of cloth or woven pattern. Bring swatches of material, easily available from any seamstress. Men and women can readily identify themselves as corduroy or bold plaids, for example, flowered cotton or creamy lace. The same response holds true for themes such as the "Tree of Life" (identify with a species of tree) or "Streams of Living Water" (provide pictures of crashing ocean waves, quiet brooks, pleasant lakes, and other examples of bodies of water). When people verbalize why they are in some way similar to an oak tree or muddy pond, they may remind themselves of their own creativity and their own self-image.

Listing Memories

An easy next step is to let people list memories associated with the tree or piece of cloth they choose. This process also stimulates recall of the past. For most people, the very act of writing—whether with pen, type-writer, or computer—unleashes memories or ideas that may have been forgotten.

Writing Thoughts to Significant Others

One simple approach to keeping a journal is writing unexpressed thoughts to people significant in one's own life. These may take the form of a letter and could well touch on unfinished business or painful episodes that were never closed. In journaling retreats I have helped conduct, we often discuss whether or not to mail the letters. While ac-knowledging the uniqueness of each situation that makes offering a flat yes or no answer impossible, I stress the truth of God's grace. As we recognize the need for healing old wounds, we discover fresh reason for depending on God's goodness and love.

Creating Prayers

Another natural way to use a journal is for writing prayers. Most people belonging to churches report that they pray, but a smaller number indicate that they have actually written down prayer ideas. Simply keeping a prayer list is a vital way to organize prayerful petitions. Because prayer also includes elements of adoration, thanksgiving, and commitment, a prayer journal can be much more inclusive than a catalog of supplications.

Ann Broyles in her book *Journaling: A Spirit Journey* gives helpful suggestions for ways to journal in response to life.[8] She encourages readers to write out reactions to important conversations they have had. She also sees journals as places to record thoughts triggered by other people's writings. Such thoughts could include responses to quotations from any source. In the context of faith exploration, such quotations appropriately come from sources including the Bible, hymns, and devotional poetry, but that is only the beginning of possibilities. A somewhat more elusive approach to journal writing mentioned by Broyles is to write in response to dreams. This idea may intimidate some people, but dreaming is a healthy reminder that we are not fully in charge of the thoughts in our minds. We are products of subconscious activity.

Benefits of Keeping a Journal

Unlike writing intended for publication or even for sharing family memoirs, journals are usually private documents not intended for other people to read. This can free the writer to be open, candid, and spontaneous. Most older people carry with them their dread from school days of being graded or judged. This dread, incidentally, may also color ideas about God as supreme Judge and Grade-giver.

At a journal-writing retreat—assuming there is a safe, caring environment—participants may feel free to share some of their writing. This is not a time to critique passages but rather to affirm the writer. Knowing that others accept us, no matter what we write, is in itself a growth-in-faith experience.

Even as we keep journals with the idea that others will not judge us, we do well to avoid self-chastisement in journal writing. Confessions and gut-level expressions are certainly in keeping with the authentic recording of self, but these private pages are not intended for self-inflicted verbal wounds.

Value of Rereading a Journal

Although the writing of thoughts and feelings in a journal is beneficial, perhaps of equal importance is the act of reviewing journal pages at a later date. Looking at my handwriting months, even years after putting entries in my journal, I have a strong sense of reconnecting with myself. When I read about the suffering and death of a colleague, I remember that I made it through that tough time of loss. When I discover passages filled with excitement about unexpected letters received from a nephew in Japan, I relive the delight of that earlier surprise.

Often my own journal writing incorporates elements of prayer. In times of need I plead to God. When I review those petitions, I recognize ways in which God's guidance led me through times of crisis. Prayers of gratitude pepper my pages. Occasionally I even insert a bold AMEN! Thus, my journal becomes a history of my own faith journey.

Interviewing Older People

For some people speaking is easier than writing. Congregations can harvest wisdom from their elders by arranging for interview sessions. When younger people talk with older people, so much the better! Elders have great insights to share.

To help people review their faith experiences, discuss questions related to the following topics. Some of these are adapted ideas from *Wellsprings* by Anthony de Mello.[9]

- Experiences I have cherished from childhood to present time
  People enshrined in my heart
  Ideas promoting sense of liberation
  Beliefs I have outgrown
  Convictions I have lived for

- Areas of life where I have gained insights
  Insights into God
  Insights into the world
  Insights into human nature
  Insights into love

- Influences that have shaped my life
  People
  Occupations
  Books/movies/television/music/art
  Events

- Risks I have taken—dangers I have courted

- Sufferings that have seasoned me

- Biblical insights that have provided light for my journey

- Achievements of which I am proud

- Areas of regret about my life

- Lessons that life has taught me

- Losses leading to learnings
  Loss of material possessions (relinquishing home, giving up car)
  Loss of abilities to function (changes in hearing, seeing, mobility)
  Loss of relationships (death of spouse, child, parent, divorce)
  Loss of dreams (what might have been)

Focusing on Faith

How can we reinforce the value of recalling and recording stories as a means for spiritual growth? Storytelling and journal writing have become popularized concepts in our culture. When browsing through bookstores or gift shops, I am often amazed at the storehouse of beautifully bound books with blank pages. Someone is making a lot of money on blank paper. But that very paper, or sheets in a budget-priced spiral notebook, can record fascinating faith journeys. Admittedly, there is no guarantee that telling or writing memories will connect one with the Holy. Congregations have a golden opportunity here to guide senior members in recognizing God's presence in their lives.

Two specific sources offer valuable insights for cultivating faith stories, one by Presbyterian minister Richard Morgan and the other by Rabbi Zalman Schacter-Shalomi. Morgan's book, *Remembering Your Story*, guides each reader in developing a spiritual autobiography.[10] In addition to incorporating a workbook style with blanks for the user's response, he also includes in each chapter devotional materials such as litanies and prayers. A leader's guide accompanies this ten-week study for those who want to pursue it in groups. An encouraging optimism permeates the pages of Morgan's volume.

> Retirement years can provide precious time to cultivate the inner life, but we persist in cramming our days full of endless activities in an attempt to wallpaper the empty spaces within. These years hold the promise of being our best years, years when we live life to the fullest. Yet often they end in depression, meaninglessness, and a gnawing sense that we are simply waiting for death. One way out of this spiritual wasteland is to discover the meaning of our life by remembering our story, connecting with God's story, and listening to another's story.[11]

Further information about the author's approach to spiritual auto-biographies appears as one of this chapter's Engaging Examples.

In *From Age-ing to Sage-ing: A Profound New Vision of Growing Older*, authors Zalman Schacter-Shalomi and Ronald Miller give us tools for cultivating wisdom and understanding in later years.[12] Through step-by-step exercises, the authors explain how to transform natural regrets, depression, and sense of loss into renewed purpose and inner peace. By elevating elderhood to a position of high regard and restoring to the aging their roles as healers and sages, these writers portray older people as precious gifts of God

Sharing the Harvest

Our technological age offers exciting means for harvesting stories. How can we preserve these unique memories? We can use tape recorders or video cameras. We can organize a visit of confirmation class members to older people, bringing questions about church and faith experiences over the decades. Many retired people work on computers. Doing so may produce faster results than writing stories in longhand. Relationships established through the Internet may lead to sharing autobiographies.

What happens to these stories after they are recalled? Encourage people to tell episodes as part of worship. Gather accounts, possibly centered around a theme such as memories of Easter or Christmas, and print them for use by the congregation. Play the audio- or videotapes at meetings. Make extra tapes to send to family members or close friends who live at a distance. Look for fresh ways to affirm life stories that celebrate a relationship with God through life's mountains and valleys.

Engaging Examples

Legacy of Faith

Under the leadership of Isabel Docampo, Calvary Baptist Church in Washington, D.C., embarked on a significant mission that combined the story of the congregation's history with faith statements from its oldest members. In this predominantly African-American church, sixty percent of the members are in later years. A large number have belonged to this same fellowship for decades. Encouraged by staff and volunteers with professional experience, these older members agreed to be videotaped as they shared their insights.

Those responsible for carrying out the Legacy of Faith project realized that it would have at least three benefits: it would clarify basic beliefs, revisit the church's history, and deepen the camaraderie among participants. The basic process involved three sessions with senior members. Each of the forty participants appeared on camera, giving his or her name and stating reasons for joining Calvary Baptist Church. Each session focused on a specific topic; for instance, at one taping session those present described what for them was a particularly meaningful ministry in their church. These descriptions led to recollections about why and how special ministries developed.

Because these sessions were held in private homes, an informal, relaxed atmosphere prevailed. Participants arrived mid-morning with bag lunches and remained until afternoon. This extended period of time allowed the storytellers to reminisce at a leisurely pace. Memories of the past surfaced that in some cases had not been recalled for many years. Recollections of how the church faced the challenge of integration produced strong emotions. But by retracing their stories participants realized how they had grown spiritually. Not surprisingly, those meeting in homes learned much about each other that was otherwise not possible to learn during superficial greetings on a Sunday or in other relatively formal settings.

This project did not stop with a backward look. At a retreat open to the entire congregation, those present watched the resulting video that had been reduced from six hours to sixty minutes. After seeing and hearing members' thoughts, participants at the retreat began discussing what was ahead for their church. They wrestled with the question of how their congregation might change in the next ten years. Oldest members could offer valuable reflections on how they had not only survived but initiated changes. Their faith-filled statements, solidified through the "Legacy of Faith" project, inspired others and reminded all of the roots of their religion.

Contact: Isabel Docampo
Baptist Senior Adult Ministries
of the Metropolitan Washington Area, Inc.
1330 Massachusetts Ave., NW
Washington, DC 20005
(202) 628-4924

Remembering Your Story

The First Presbyterian Church in Morganton, North Carolina, is an active, growing congregation with an average worship attendance of three hundred people. Although this congregation has an aggressive program of outreach to the community and world, it has seen a decline of all ages in its Christian education programs. To combat this decline, the church offers small, elective classes to interest adults.

One of the courses offered at First Presbyterian Church is Remembering Your Story. Based on a book by the same name, this ten-week class guides students in developing their own spiritual autobiographies. They seek to discover where God is and has been at work in their lives.

Richard L. Morgan, author of this resource and one of the ministers at First Presbyterian, facilitated a group using his book. Morgan found the students responsive to linking life events with biblical stories, an effective way to help participants identify people from their past who have helped them. The book also provides a process whereby individuals can extend forgiveness to people who have wronged them.

The leader's guide has proven to be of inestimable help for lay leaders. After Morgan led the first ten-session class, two of its members became facilitators for a new group. Moreover, the church foresees other uses for the book including spiritual formation experiences for church officers, youth life stories, and intergenerational effort using youth listeners to record the life stories of older members shut in at home or in nursing facilities.

Contact: Dr. Richard L. Morgan, Parish Associate
First Presbyterian Church
Morganton, North Carolina 28655
(704) 437-4498

Points to Ponder

1. In what ways is your congregation encouraging older people to develop faith stories?

- Presenting faith stories during worship?
- Organizing groups for reminiscing?
- Printing stories of members' faith experiences?

2. What kinds of pastoral counseling does your congregation provide for those whose memories of unresolved, painful experiences contribute to depression?

3. How does or could your congregation foster the sharing of faith stories from one generation to another?

4. If your congregation has a historian, how does that person interact with older people?

5. What resources are there in your community for helping older residents sharpen their writing and documenting skills?

6. Which members in your congregation could assist with a project related to spiritual autobiographies?

- Presenting the idea?
- Developing a means of "harvesting wisdom"?
- Promoting the concept among the senior population?
- Giving technical assistance through audiotaping, videotaping, or in other ways helping people who have difficulty in writing memoirs?

7. How does or might your congregation honor older members who want to share their spiritual autobiographies?

CHAPTER 10

Dwelling – Home Is Where . . .

Importance of Home

"Where do you live?" Knowing the answer to that question is one of the basic tasks of early childhood. Every form or survey we complete, from magazine subscriptions to income tax returns, asks for our address. Young people just leaving the nest launch out on their own to establish their first homes, a significant move into maturity. In later years, people may feel that their empty nest is too big, that maintaining a house is too much responsibility. A primary decision at any stage in life is deciding where to reside.

For years the American ideal included a "chicken in every pot" and "a car in every garage." Buying one's own home represented stability and financial security, and was usually a considerable investment involving mortgage payments over many years. But neighborhoods change and older houses often require costly maintenance. The treasured family home may in later years present a staggering range of new problems.

In answering the question "Where shall I live?" this chapter will review various options for living arrangements in the context of how congregations deal with housing concerns. Churches and synagogues in communities of every size and location no doubt have older members in any or all of these categories:

- those who want to remain in their own homes
- those who need help in caring for older people living with them
- those who require respite assistance or specialized services such as adult day care

- those who are seeking guidance in selecting a long-term care facility for themselves or others

Because home is where we spend so much of our time, the topic of housing pervades practically every other aspect of life choices. The matter of where one lives relates to a number of subjects mentioned in earlier chapters. Continuing education may in part depend on proximity of libraries, community colleges, and senior centers. Smaller communities may not offer as many social welfare agencies as do larger communities, but residents may develop informal support systems that function effectively. Health care services in rural areas may differ widely from sophisticated technology available in large cities. Even access to religious activities depends to some extent on where one lives and what transportation is available.

As we recognize the importance of home, we may become more sensitive to the enormous issues related to where older people live.

Aging in Place

The phrase "aging in place" is now commonly used to indicate that aging people want to stay where they are. As Harriet Kerr Swenson observes, "No adjustment is more difficult to the older adult than moving to a new place of residence where new persons and unaccustomed space become home."[1] A major survey conducted in 1989 by AARP revealed that 86 percent of those interviewed wanted to stay in their present home and never move.[2] In what ways, then, can congregations assist the elderly who need help to remain in their own homes?

When desire for independence burns fiercely in anyone, that person may deny situations or conditions that make independence unrealistic. My own father in later years insisted that he was capable of driving a car, even after he shifted incorrectly and rammed through the front of his garage. As we become aware of living conditions and the resident's ability to function at home, we may determine if the congregation can offer help in any of the following situations:

- assisting with transportation, especially driving to medical appointments

- shopping for groceries, either taking the person to the store or taking the shopping list and buying the needed items for the person
- checking for safety features in an older person's home, such as grab bars in the bathroom and nonskid throw rugs on the floor
- assessing a person's ability to prepare meals, manage medications and personal hygiene, dress, and manage other activities of daily living.

The above checklist suggests the value of having either a formal or informal system in the congregation to provide services such as shopping, transporting, and doing simple chores around the house. Is there a youth group that can occasionally do yard work? Are there handy people skilled in home repairs who can install deadbolt safety locks? Perhaps most important, is a staff person or volunteer knowledgeable about community resources? The phrase "When you care you are aware" reminds us of the need to be informed about struggles people may be having. Without infringing on the privacy rights of others, we can be alert to changing needs and ways to respond in caring, loving ways.

With whom do older people confer when they deliberate about housing options? According to the AARP survey cited earlier, only 12 percent of older people consulted anyone else about their decision.[3] The majority of people they did consult were children, grandchildren, or other family members. Only 3 percent of those wanting guidance talked with a clergyperson about this decision. In my estimation this suggests that clergy are not seen as vital sources of housing information, and such a finding is not too surprising.

Realizing that family members are often embroiled in discussing where parents or grandparents will live, clergy do well to connect with the various generations. One alternative to suggest is the concept of shared housing. The idea of several older unrelated people living in the same home sounds appealing. Eating together, splitting cost of utilities, having a companion for socialization—all these appear to be advantages. In my experience, however, an older woman may want someone to come live in her house, but she probably is not willing to go live in someone else's house. Creating a congenial match requires wisdom and patience.

Employing someone to come into the home could be costly but it might also be the determining factor for "aging in place." The Church Council of Greater Seattle Task Force on Aging has excellent guidance

in this matter. In a booklet titled "How to Hire Helpers," the Task Force
outlines how to develop a job description and contract, what steps to
take in advertising and interviewing, plus legal and financial considerations of which to be aware.[4] Caring committees in congregations would
benefit from becoming acquainted with such a document.

But in what ways do churches and synagogues extend spiritual
nurture to people in their homes, especially persons who may be frail?
People unable to attend worship with their congregations often find deep
comfort and support through receiving the sacraments in their home.
Eucharistic visitors in the Roman Catholic Church regularly take communion to homebound people. Audio- or videotapes of worship services, even typed copies of sermons, enable people in their homes to
feel closer to the congregation. Devotional guides take on additional
meaning when the reader knows that friends are meditating with the
same passages.

Phone calls and personal visits are an essential part of ministry.
One highly developed approach for lay visitation used by churches of
many denominations is called Stephen Ministry. Congregations engaged
in the Stephen Ministry program recognize the importance of thorough
preparation for such contacts. Additional resources for equipping pastoral caring teams include books such as *If There's Anything I Can Do
for You* and *A Ministry of Caregiving*.[5] No matter if the church member
is living at home or in a congregate setting, contact with the home
church is vital for feeling part of the faith community.

Moving In with a Relative

When remaining in one's own home is no longer a viable option, one
alternative may be for the older generation to move in with adult children or other relatives. Reasons prompting such a consideration include
inability of the older person to manage medications, difficulty in buying
and preparing food, struggles in maintaining own property, extreme
depression or other mental health concerns, and the death of a partner.

A move that involves changing communities may pose special challenges. One question to consider is how to help the older person establish new relationships. Leaving what is familiar, whether that be a
favorite shopping area, neighbors, medical personnel, or church, can be

traumatic. In some cases the grandparent generation has been active in a local congregation. How will he or she develop new friendships in a strange location? Making such a transition requires creative approaches on the part of congregations and all generations.

Whatever the geographical setting, adding an older adult to a household necessitates patient, prayerful preparation. Author Sheelagh McGurn in her book *Under One Roof* deals openly with the realities of caring for an aging parent.[6] Addressing the fears that may smolder in all involved, McGurn emphasizes the importance of raising basic questions before attempting any move:

- What will be the financial implications?
- How much physical care will be required?
- What if personality clashes arise?
- In what ways will the move affect not only the adult child but that person's spouse and children and any other members of household?
- Will family pets be an issue?
- Are there issues of values and religious beliefs to consider?

Having several generations under the same roof can have important advantages. In some settings the grandfather assists with simple gardening. Older women may want to contribute by helping with baking and other kitchen tasks. Family stories and traditions revive or come alive when older and younger ages celebrate holidays or other special times. Generations can also grow spiritually as they intentionally take time to pray together and nurture their souls as well as their bodies. Church and synagogue members must be alert to stresses experienced by each age level. Emotional reactions, such as anger and guilt, may be suppressed. Those skilled in pastoral care will want to note deep feelings that need to be acknowledged and explored.

Congregate Living Alternatives

Sometimes personal and family situations dictate that an older person or couple move to a setting where help is available. Many communities are experimenting with informal as well as formal housing options. The descriptions below are for the most part commonly provided alternatives.

Any level can be sponsored by congregations. Each church and synagogue needs to know what is available or needed in its community.

Board and Care Homes

A growing trend is for owners of private homes to serve older people for a fee. These community-based residences provide room and board, assistance with activities of daily living such as bathing, dressing, grooming, and some degree of protective supervision. Such homes vary in size, resident mix, services, ownership, management, location, and cost. Government regulating bodies, whether municipal, county, or state, have differing standards for licensing or accreditation.

Assisted Living

A comparatively new, widely used term is *assisted living*. The basic philosophy of assisted living emphasizes the autonomy of residents. This residential care model combines private apartment-style living with services such as grooming, bathing, and dressing. Living units must be private with full bath and some equipment for food preparation. Many of these living units resemble studio apartments.

Because independence is prized so highly in this model, residents often participate in helping to design their own care plan. Privacy rights rank high as a priority. A consumer guide from AARP states, "The trade-off between greater autonomy and safety in assisted living has given rise to a concept called managed or negotiated risk. In effect, under such policies the resident may decide to accept greater risk of personal injury or loss in exchange for greater freedom."[7]

Multilevel Retirement Centers

An increasingly popular choice for senior adults contemplating a move from their private residence is that of entering a retirement facility that has various levels of care. These levels may include so-called independent living in self-contained apartments, an intermediate level that might be assisted living, and a skilled nursing care unit. Many of these complexes, especially those sponsored by religious bodies, are members of the American Association of Homes and Services for the Aging (AAHSA). This association of over five thousand nonprofit homes, housing projects, health-related facilities, and community services includes many outstanding institutions with sectarian affiliation.

Although the older facilities related to AAHSA may still function strictly on the basis of monthly fees for services, a growing number are classified as continuing care retirement communities (CCRCs). These CCRCs, in exchange for providing full or life care, usually require a sizeable investment. At the time of entrance, residents may be functioning very well, able to care for their own apartments or cottages and may still be active in the wider community. Later, if a resident's physical or mental capacities change, the CCRC facility is obligated to provide additional services and care.

Based on my personal involvements with multilevel facilities, I can testify to several advantages over traditional, freestanding nursing homes. When my parents moved into the Beatitudes Campus of Care, described later in this chapter, they lived quite independently in a garden apartment. Whenever they chose to do so, they could eat in the attractive main dining room. By participating in activities such as the campus choral group or the Kiwanis Club, they developed firm friendships. Positive contacts with other residents and staff eased their transition from independent living to other levels when they needed nursing help. After my father's transfer to the care center where he received skilled nursing, my mother could spend a good portion of each day with him. Although living in different buildings, they were still on the same property. Another source of satisfaction to my parents was sharing in church-related opportunities such as study groups led by clergy, weekly services coordinated by the chaplain, and frequent visits from church volunteers.

Selecting a Nursing Home or Retirement Facility

Choosing a final residence for retirement years is a major decision with physical, spiritual, emotional, and financial implications. This choice is certainly as important as deciding which college to attend, and people ordinarily spend more years living in a retirement home than they do going to college. Most high schools have college counselors to help

students explore possible choices. Where can retirees turn for advice?
Why not equip congregations to assist with this life-shaping choice?
    Key questions to help retirees ask include:

- How important is it to be near family members?
- What would be gained and what would be lost in moving to another
  community or state?
- What kinds of leisure activities are available?
- In what ways is the facility connected to the wider world?
- By which organizations is this facility accredited?
- How appealing is the physical setting?
- What seems to be the preparation and morale of the staff?
- What provisions are there for intellectual and spiritual nurture?
- How much will it cost to live in this facility?

Helping Congregations Relate to Members in Long-term Care Facilities

When members of our churches and synagogues enter nursing homes or
other institutions, how do we make certain that they do not become
"invisible elderly"? Here are a few examples of ways churches maintain
healthy, caring relationships with those individuals.
    Continuing communication is primary. Keeping these people on the
regular mailing list will help them know they are not forgotten. Many
churches, such as a Roman Catholic parish in New Orleans, assign volunteers to be partnered with members in nursing homes. These volunteers may visit weekly, delivering the order of worship and perhaps
audiotapes of the worship service. One bedridden woman in this parish
reportedly spent much of each week studying the latest bulletin, checking the names of each person mentioned by looking them up in the
church's pictorial directory. This same resident also devoted hours to
praying for each person mentioned in the bulletin.
    Transgenerational caring includes having children adopt nursing
home residents as pen pals. Because some frail elderly are unable to
write easily, the idea of phone pals may be substituted. Before involving
elementary school children in such a project, it is helpful to have them
visit their "pal." Wise teachers will make careful preparations to help

educate children about life in a nursing center and some of the limitations residents experience. Young people can also learn to appreciate the strengths and gifts of the aging.

Even clergy may need help in knowing how best to relate to parishioners experiencing multiple losses. A valuable resource for anyone who visits on behalf of a congregation is *With God's Oldest Friends: Pastoral Visiting in the Nursing Home.* In a very direct manner the authors, Henry C. Simmons and Mark A. Peters, discuss basic guidelines for nursing home visitation. Chapters focus on topics such as communicating with Alzheimer's patients, using sacraments and rituals, and the trauma involved in leaving one's own home when entering a nursing home. "Whatever the benefits of physical care in this new setting, the human spirit is likely to be stirred by anger toward the family and God, a sense of uselessness, and a highly personal and threatening loneliness."[8]

Those responsible for visitation first need to acknowledge the many negative feelings surging through residents. Too often there is a tendency for callers to deny a resident's despair; superficial cheeriness only leads the resident to more agony. In misdirected efforts to ignore spiritual pain, those of us who are outsiders may rush in with quick fix ideas such as urging residents to participate in every available activity. In some cases, participation in activities may be therapeutic. Elderly people living in nursing homes report, however, that what helps them adapt to new surroundings more than anything is personal prayer.

As members of congregations learn to feel comfortable visiting elders who are frail, those elders can enrich the faith community with testimonies of their faith. *With God's Oldest Friends*, the book mentioned earlier, provides useful insights.

> Nursing home residents have much to teach us. If we are unafraid to draw close, we have much to learn and thus to preach. The lessons have pointedness that gives new meaning to religious convictions that all life is holy, and is part of God's gift.... While life is gifted, it is also burdened by its fickleness. The nursing home resident who has learned anew to thank God for this life can be a powerful teacher and witness.[9]

Another role for congregations to play is in the arena of advocacy.

Sometimes clergy or other visitors will discover that residents' rights are being abused. If, after gathering all available facts, there is indeed abuse, then investigation is in order. By contacting your area agency on aging, you can find out how to reach an ombudsman, a professional designated to help protect residents. Unfortunately, elder abuse can occur in any setting—in one's own home, in board and room facilities, and even in the fanciest retirement center. Our challenge is to speak up on behalf of those who feel mistreated. Ideally, homes affiliated with religious organizations emphasize the need for staff and volunteers to offer caring, competent services.

Often we speak of churches, synagogues, and temples as "houses of God." Such a phrase reminds us that we are all pilgrims journeying through this life, supporting each other during this pilgrimage. Our need for a different type of residence may change, but the essence of who we are goes with us from place to place. And we can reassure one another that at the end, "I shall dwell in the house of the Lord forever." (Psalm 23:6b)

Engaging Examples

Beatitudes Campus of Care

One of the major distinctions about this premier retirement campus is that just one congregation built and administers it. Church of the Beatitudes, affiliated with the United Church of Christ, had its birth in 1954. Only six years after organizing, lay leaders and clergy determined that the community needed decent housing for retirees. Even as it was beginning to construct its own space for worship and education, this fledgling congregation established as a priority the development of a multilevel retirement facility. Guidelines for pursuing this massive project included building the campus less than a mile from the church and keeping it affordable for the broad middle-class population.

By 1965 residents began occupying the first of two high-rise apartment buildings. In the next few years the major housing units were completed: 64 garden apartments; 273 apartments in twin, five-story buildings; and the lodge containing assisted living and intermediate care, as well as the care center offering skilled nursing care.

This home for some seven hundred residents has the usual comple-
ment of professional staff and services: social workers, nursing teams,
food service, housekeeping, therapists, chaplain, activities directors,
hospice services, beauty and barber shops, full-service bank, ice cream
parlor with groceries, maintenance, plus an array of administrative
personnel.

Especially impressive to me is the close relationship maintained
between the campus and Church of the Beatitudes located just one-half
mile away. The chief executive officer of the campus is also a member
of the church clergy team. Campus and church staff meet together on a
regular basis. One of the goals for these meetings is to continue enhancing ways that the two facilities can interact. Here are a few examples of
significant interactions.

- Youth from the church help sell refreshments at the annual fall flea
  market.
- Children's choirs sing on the campus for special events.
- Through the work of parish nurses, the congregation works with the
  campus chaplain in establishing a support group for people receiving
  treatment for cancer.
- The board of directors for the Campus of Care is in essence an official
  ministry of the church. Most of the directors are church members.
- Food service from the campus caters meal events at the church,
  including the monthly meetings of Friendly Adults, a social group for
  retired people.
- The campus chaplain and Religious Life Committee develop seasonal
  worship services, such as Thanksgiving, Christmas, and Good Friday,
  to which the congregation is invited. At some of these services the
  campus choir sings.

Beatitudes Center D.O.A.R.

When the campus had been operating fifteen years, one of the clergy
serving both the campus and the church became increasingly aware of
older church members living in the community who wanted to remain in
their own homes. Some of these elderly men and women choosing to age
in place could no longer do their own shopping or perform certain

household chores. In response to such needs the church and campus organized another ministry, the Beatitudes Center for Developing Older Adult Resources (Center D.O.A.R.).

Center D.O.A.R. quickly grew into a flourishing interfaith endeavor with four specialized programs:

- Flinn Learning Resource Center, housing a circulating library and educational events
- GENERATIONS, offering referral services and support groups for caregivers, including grandparents raising grandchildren
- Nurse Ministries Network, assisting congregations to promote health and well-being through the work of parish nurses
- Volunteer Interfaith Caregivers Program, coordinating informal support services for caregivers and homebound and disabled people through volunteers from the community and nearly ninety congregations, including Catholic, Jewish, Protestant, and Orthodox groups.

Age Link

In 1996 the Campus of Care broke ground for the emerging Beatitudes Age Link. This is an intergenerational child development center adjoining the campus intentionally designed to bring youngest and oldest generations together. Again, a campus-church partnership strengthened the program. Community participants, such as the Junior League of Phoenix, eagerly contributed leadership and financial support. Residents from the campus share their expertise in areas such as gardening, music, cooking, crafts, and drama.

While some churches may choose not to become so involved in aging ministries as Church of the Beatitudes, portions of their ministry are certainly easily replicated.

Contact: Dr. Kenneth Buckwald, Chief Executive Officer
Beatitudes Campus of Care
1610 West Glendale Ave.
Phoenix, AZ 85021
(602) 995-2611

Elizabeth Brunstein, Executive Director
Beatitudes Center for Developing Older Adult Resources
555 West Glendale Ave.
Phoenix, AZ 85021
(602) 274-5022

Main Line Adult Day Center

Although congregations have long been involved in day care programs for young children, they have only recently begun serving older people who need assistance during the day. Bryn Mawr Presbyterian Church in Pennsylvania offers one outstanding example of this kind of ministry. In 1989 this congregation established a non-profit corporation that operates their Main Line Adult Day Center. The church owns a recently enlarged house that accommodates forty-four participants.

Five days a week this center offers participants a safe, supportive, homelike atmosphere. Adults who may be physically or cognitively impaired can enjoy group and individual activities, hot lunches, snacks, and special diets. Paid staff and volunteers assist with basic tasks of daily living such as toileting and communication skills. Professional personnel, in addition to giving guidance to the enrolled member, also counsel the caregivers and other family members. A significant selling point for families is that this type of care can prevent inappropriate or premature institutionalization.

Additional benefits of such a program are numerous. Men and women who might otherwise be isolated at home can interact with peers and staff. Caregivers, many of them employed adult children, know their relative or friend is safe. Such assurance brings relief and respite to those constant caregivers. Consider the satisfaction a daughter or son feels who might otherwise have to spend twenty-four hours a day caring for a parent who has had a stroke or who is exhibiting some form of dementia.

Establishing a day care setting may be challenging. Licensing requirements that vary from state to state usually mandate that there be trained staff conducting adult day care programs. State and county officials conduct periodic inspections. Even when congregations donate use of building space, there are personnel costs and other programming expenses. Using church and community volunteers can help reduce the budget. Although the Bryn Mawr center charges a fee for participation, they are able to make adjustments for those of limited income. Scholarship aid from the church makes the difference. A 501(C)3 non-profit corporation, this center has directors from both the congregation and the wider community.

Churches or synagogues interested in exploring day care for adults may want to begin with a limited schedule, being open perhaps only one day a week. If the project seems too demanding for a single congregation, this may be an excellent mission to share with other congregations and social agencies. The need for adult day care will no doubt keep increasing in years ahead. What a great opportunity this presents for skillful innovators who want to put faith in action by responding to this need.

Adult day care is only one engaging example at Bryn Mawr Presbyterian Church. Thanks to a multimillion dollar grant, this church showcases an outstanding ministry for older adults with two full-time paid staff and scores of volunteers. Samuel Riccobene, Associate Pastor for Older Adult Ministry, describes four dimensions of programming: spirituality, education, socialization, and outreach, all coordinated by the forty-member Older Adults Council. Although this well-funded, extensive operation is atypical among churches, separate programs can be replicated in other settings. Even a listing of selected projects will suggest ideas for consideration: mission work trips, tutoring in surrounding communities, medical equipment lending closet, audiovisual personal histories, walking club, large print and hearing aid ministry, telephone conference call devotions, spirituality groups. And the list is even longer! Contact the church for details.

Contact: Nina Maschak, Director
Main Line Adult Day Center
119 Radnor Street
Bryn Mawr, PA 19010-3506
(215) 527-4220

Samuel Riccobene, Associate Pastor for Older Adult Ministry
Bryn Mawr Presbyterian Church
625 Montgomery Ave.
Bryn Mawr, PA 19010
(610) 525-2821

Points to Ponder

1. Sharing stories about where we have lived can elicit powerful memories, both positive and negative. Discuss this topic with older adults.

2. Who in your congregation is well informed about social services that may enable people to "age in place"?

3. What provisions does your congregation have for offering spiritual nurture to members who are homebound or in nursing homes?

4. Do you know elderly people who have moved in with adult children or other relatives? What have been the advantages and disadvantages?

5. In what ways is "negotiated risk" a theological issue? How might an obsession with personal rights and independence contradict religious values?

6. How does your church presently relate to members living in nursing homes? What additional forms of contact and support might you develop?

7. Ponder the importance of an ombudsman. Check the provisions in your community for such advocacy services.

Addresses

American Association of Homes and Services for the Aging
901 E. Street NW, Suite 500
Washington, DC 20004
(202) 783-2242

American Association of Retired Persons
601 E. Street, NW
Washington, DC 20049
(202) 434-6070

American Society on Aging
833 Market Street, Suite 512
San Francisco, CA 94103
(415) 442-0434

Beatitudes Center for Developing Older Adult Resources
555 W. Glendale Avenue
Phoenix, AZ 85021
(602) 274-5022

Bi-Folkal Productions, Inc.
809 Williamson Street
Madison, WI 53703
(800) 568-5357

Center for Aging, Religion, and Spirituality
2481 Como Avenue
St. Paul, MN 55108
(612) 641-3581

Center on Rural Elderly
5245 Rockhill Road
Kansas City, MO 64110
(816) 235-1024

Church Council of Greater Seattle
4759 15th NE
Seattle, WA 98105
(206) 285-4589

Congregational Ministries Division
Presbyterian Church (U.S.A.)
100 Witherspoon Street, Room 2008
Louisville KY 40202-1396
(502) 569-5487

Elderhostel
75 Federal Street
Boston, MA 02110-1941
(617) 426-8056

Episcopal Society for Ministry on Aging
323 Wyandotte
Bethlehem, PA 18015
(610) 868-5400

Federal Domestic Volunteer Agency
Washington, DC 20525

Forum on Religion, Spirituality and Aging
American Society on Aging
833 Market Street, Suite 511
San Francisco, CA 94103-1824
(415) 974-9600

Generations Together
University of Pittsburgh
121 University Place, Suite 300
Pittsburgh, PA 15260
(412) 648-7150

Generations United:
A National Coalition on Intergenerational Issues and Programs
c/o Child Welfare League of America
440 First Street, NW, Suite 310
Washington, DC 20001
(202) 638-2952

Healing Community: The Caring Congregation
521 Harrison Avenue
Claremont, CA 91711
(909) 621-6808

Health and Economic Justice Working Group
c/o Edgewood United Church
469 N. Hagadorn Road
East Lansing, MI 48823
(517) 332-8693

International Parish Nurse Resource Center
205 W. Touhy, Suite 104
Park Ridge, IL 60068
(800) 556-5368

National Association of Area Agencies on Aging
1112 16th Street, NW, Suite 100
Washington, DC 20036
(202) 296-8130

National Council on the Aging, Inc.
409 Third Street, SW, Suite 200
Washington, DC 20024
(202) 479-1200

National Federation of Interfaith Volunteer Caregivers
368 Broadway, Suite 103
Box 1939
Kingston, NY 12401
(914) 331-1358

National Hospice Organization
1901 N. Moore Street, Suite 901
Arlington, VA 22209
(800) 658-8898

National Interfaith Coalition on Aging
National Council on the Aging
409 Third Street, SW
Washington, DC 20024
(202) 479-1200

National Organization on Disablity
9100 16th Street, NW, Suite 600
Washington, DC 20006
(202) 293-5960

National Shared Housing Resource Center
St. Ambrose Housing Aid Center
321 E. 25th Street
Baltimore, MD 21218
(410) 235-4454

Older Women's League
666 Eleventh Street, NW, Suite 700
Washington, DC 20001
(202) 783-6686

Otterbein Home
585 North Street
State Road 741
Lebanon, OH 45036-9551
(513) 932-2020

Presbyterian Older Adult Ministry Network
Presbyterian Church (U.S.A.)
100 Witherspoon Street
Louisville, KY 40202-1396
(502) 569-5487

Retired and Senior Volunteer Program
12201 New York Avenue, NW
Washington, DC 20525
(202) 606-5000
525

Shalem Institute for Spiritual Formation
Mount St. Alban
Washington, DC 20016
(202) 966-7050

Shepherd's Centers of America
6700 Troost, Suite 616
Kansas City, MO 64131-4401
(816) 523-1080

Spiritual Directors International (has list of all known programs)
2300 Adeline Drive
Burlingame, CA 94010-5599
(415) 340-7483

Spiritual Eldering Institute
7318 Germantown Avenue
Philadelphia, PA 19919
(215) 242-4074

Spiritual Formation Programs
Scarritt-Bennett Center
1008 19th Avenue S.
Nashville, TN 37212-2166
(615) 340-7557

Temple University Center for Intergenerational Learning
1601 N. Broad Street, Room 206
Philadelphia, PA 19122
(215) 204-6836

United Church of Sun City
11250 N. 107th Avenue
Sun City, AZ 85351
(606) 933-0058

Volunteer Interfaith Caregivers Program
555 W. Glendale Avenue
Phoenix, AZ 85021
(602) 285-0543

Bibliography

Berman, Harry. *Interpreting the Aging Self: Personal Journals in Later Life*. New York: Springer Publishing Company, Inc., 1994.

Berman, Phillip L., and Connie Goldman, eds. *The Ageless Spirit*. New York: Ballantine Books, 1992.

Bianchi, Eugene. *Aging as a Spiritual Journey*. New York: Crossroad Publishing Company, 1984.

Birren, James E., and Donna E. Deutchman. *Guiding Autobiography Groups for Older Adults*. Baltimore: Johns Hopkins University Press, 1991.

Broyles, Ann. *Journaling: A Spirit Journey*. Nashville: Upper Room Books, 1988.

Cameron, Julia, and Mark Bryan. *The Artist's Way: A Spiritual Path to Higher Creativity*. New York: G. P. Putnam's Sons, 1992.

Carlsen, Mary Baird. *Creative Aging: A Meaning-Making Perspective*. New York: W. W. Norton and Company, 1991.

Claman, Victor N., and David E.Butler with Jessica A.Boyatt. *Acting on Your Faith: Congregations Making a Difference*. Boston: Insights, 1994.

Cohen, Lee, ed. *Justice across Generations*. Washington, D.C.: American Association of Retired Persons, 1993.

de Mello, Anthony, S.J. *Wellsprings: A Book of Spiritual Exercises*. New York: Doubleday, 1985.

Dychtwald, Ken. *Age Wave*. Los Angeles: Jeremy P. Tarcher, Inc., 1989.

Fischer, Kathleen. *Winter Grace: Spirituality for the Later Years*. New York: Paulist Press, 1985.

————. *Autumn Gospel*. New York: Paulist Press, 1995.

Gentzler, Richard H., and Donald F. Clingan. *Aging: God's Challenge to Church and Synagogue*. Nashville: Discipleship Resources, 1996.

Herbert, Trish. *The Vintage Years: A Guide to Artful Aging*. Cleveland: United Church Press, 1995.

Kavanaugh, Patrick. *Spiritual Lives of Great Composers*. Grand Rapids, Mich.: Zondervan Publishing House, 1996.

Kimble, Melvin A., ed., with James W. Ellor, Susan H. McFadden, and James J. Seeber. *Aging, Religion, and Spirituality: A Handbook*. Minneapolis: Fortress Press, 1995.

Lukens, Joan E., ed. *Affirmative Aging: A Creative Approach to Longer Life*. Harrisburg, Pa.: Morehouse Publishing, 1994.

Maves, Paul. *Older Volunteers in Church and Community: A Manual for Ministry*. Valley Forge, Pa.: Judson Press, 1981.

McMahan, Harry, and Gloria McMahan. *Grandma Was Quite a Girl: A Family Heirloom Book*. Escondido, Calif.: McMahan, 1980.

Morgan, Richard L. *Autumn Wisdom*. Nashville: Upper Room Books, 1995.

————. *No Wrinkles on the Soul*. Nashville: Upper Room Books, 1990.

————. *Remembering Your Story*. Nashville: Upper Room Books, 1996.

Older Adult Ministry: Growing in the Abundant Life. A Report Adopted by the 204th General Assembly, Presbyterian Church (U.S.A.). Louisville, Kentucky, 1992.

Peckham, Charles W., and Arline B. Peckham. *I Can Still Pray*. Lebanon, Ohio: Otterbein Home, 1979. Available through Otterbein Home listed in appendix A.

Pierskalla, Carol Spargo, and Jane Dewey Heald. *Help for Families of the Aging*. Swarthmore, Pa.: Support Source, 1988.

Sawin, Margaret. *Family Enrichment with Family Clusters*. Valley Forge, Pa.: Judson Press, 1979.

Schacter-Shalomi, Zalman, and Ronald S.Miller. *From Age-ing to Sage-ing: A Profound New Vision of Growing Older*. New York: Warner Books, Inc., 1995.

Seymour, Robert E. *Aging without Apology: Living the Senior Years with Integrity and Faith*. Valley Forge, Pa.: Judson Press, 1995.

Simmons, Henry C., and Mark A. Peters. *With God's Oldest Friends: Pastoral Visiting in the Nursing Home*. New York: Paulist Press, 1996.

Strom, Robert, and Shirley Strom. *Achieving Grandparent Potential: Viewpoints on Building Intergenerational Relationships*. Newbury Park, Calif.: Sage Publications, Inc., 1992.

————. *Becoming a Better Grandparent: Viewpoints on Strengthening the Family*. Newbury Park, Calif.: Sage Publications, Inc., 1992.

Swenson, Harriet Kerr. *Visible and Vital: A Handbook for the Aging Congregation*. New York: Paulist Press, 1994.

Takas, Marianne. *Grandparents Raising Grandchildren: A Guide to Finding Help and Hope*. New York: Brookdale Foundation Group, 1995.

Thibault, Jane Marie. *A Deepening Love Affair: The Gift of God in Later Life*. Nashville, Tenn.: Upper Room Books, 1993.

Thomas, L. Eugene, and Susan A.Eisenhandler. *Aging and the Religious Dimension*. Westport, Conn.: Auburn House, 1994.

Williams, Mark E. *American Geriatric Society's Complete Guide to Aging and Health*. New York: Harmony Books, 1995.

Wilson, Marlene. *How to Mobilize Church Volunteers*. Minneapolis: Augsburg Publishing House, 1983.

———. *You Can Make a Difference: Helping Others and Yourself through Volunteering*. Boulder, Colo.: Volunteer Management Associates, 1990.

Chapter 1

1. Joan E. Lukens, ed., *Affirmative Aging: A Creative Approach to Longer Living* (Harrisburg, Pa.: Morehouse Publishing, for The Episcopal Society for Ministry on Aging, Inc., 1994).

2. *Images of Aging in America* (Washington, D.C.: American Association of Retired Persons, Research Division, 1995).

3. Melvin A. Kimble, et al., eds., "Pastoral Care," *Aging, Spirituality, and Religion: A Handbook* (Minneapolis: Fortress Press, 1995), p. 133.

4. Lukens, *Affirmative Aging.*

5. *Older Adult Ministry: Growing in the Abundant Life* (Louisville, Ky.: Office of the General Assembly, Presbyterian Church, U.S.A., 1992), pp. 5-6.

Chapter 2

1. *Generations Together: An Intergenerational Studies Program* (Pittsburgh: University of Pittsburgh, 1994), p. 4.

2. Lee Cohen, ed., *Justice Across Generations* (Washington, D.C.: Public Policy Institute of American Association of Retired Persons, 1993).

3. Rabbi Harlan Wechsler in *Justice Across Generations*, chapter 1.

4. James M. Galliher, ed., *Directory of Intergenerational Programming.* Available from the Center on Rural Elderly listed in appendix A.

5. Doug Manning, *When Love Gets Tough: The Nursing Home Decision* (Hereford, Tex.: In-Sight Books, Inc., 1989). Katherine L. Karr, *Taking Time for Me* (Buffalo, N.Y.: Prometheus Books, 1992).

Enid Pritikin and Trudy Reece, *Parentcare Survival Guide* (Hauppage, N.Y.: Barron's, 1993). Robert W. Buckingham, *When Living Alone Means Living at Risk: A Guide for Caregivers and Families* (Buffalo, N.Y.: Prometheus Books, 1994).

6. Carol Spargo Pierskalla and Jane Dewey Heald, *Help for Families of the Aging* (Swarthmore, Pa.: Support Source, 1988).

7. "Findings from the Medicare Alzheimer's Disease Demonstration: The Rewards of Caregiving," Cheryl Schraeder, project director. Carle Clinic Association, Clinical Studies Department, Champaign-Urbana, Illinois, n.d.

8. Robert D. Strom and Shirley K. Strom, *Becoming a Better Grandparent: Strengthening the Family* (Newbury Park, Calif.: Sage Publications, 1991). Robert D. Strom and Shirley K. Strom, *Achieving Grandparent Potential: Building Intergenerational Relationships* (Newbury Park, Calif.: Sage Publications, 1992).

9. Margaret Sawin, *Family Enrichment with Family Clusters.* (Valley Forge, Pa.: Judson Press, 1979).

Chapter 3

1. Mark E. Williams, *American Geriatric Society's Complete Guide to Aging and Health* (New York: Harmony Books, 1995), p. 16.

2. Loren Mead, *Transforming Congregations for the Future* (Bethesda, Md.: The Alban Institute, 1994), p. 61.

3. National Clergy Leadership Project to Prepare for an Aging Society, *Incline Your Ear and Apply Your Mind to Knowledge* (Washington, D.C.: National Interfaith Coalition on Aging of the National Council on the Aging, Inc., 1994).

4. Materials are available through the National Council on the Aging listed in appendix A.

5. To obtain a catalog, contact Elderhostel listed in appendix A.

Chapter 4

1. NICA is now affiliated with the National Council on the Aging listed in appendix A.

2. Richard H. Gentzler, Jr. and Donald F. Clingan, *Aging: God's Challenge to Church and Synagogue* (Nashville: Discipleship Resources, 1996), p. 16. A helpful historical background of NICA can be obtained from the address listed in appendix A of this book.

3. Robert E. Seymour, *Aging without Apology: Living the Senior Years with Integrity and Faith* (Valley Forge, Pa.: Judson Press, 1995), p. 38.

4. Eugene Bianchi, *Aging as a Spiritual Journey* (New York: Crossroad Publishing Co., 1985).

5. Linda Vogel, "Spiritual Development in Later Life," in *Aging, Spirituality, and Religion*, Melvin A. Kimble, et al., eds. (Minneapolis: Fortress Press, 1995), p. 81.

6. Robert C. Atchley, "The Continuity of the Spiritual Self," in *Aging, Spirituality, and Religion*, Melvin A. Kimble, et al., eds. (Minneapolis: Fortress Press, 1995), pp. 70-71.

7. Harry Moody, "Mysticism," in *Aging, Spirituality, and Religion*, Melvin A. Kimble, et al., eds. (Minneapolis: Fortress Press, 1995), pp. 97-98.

8. Jane Marie Thibault, *A Deepening Love Affair: The Gift of God in Later Life* (Nashville: Upper Room Books, 1993).

9. C. Jeff Woods, *Congregational Megatrends* (Bethesda, Md.: The Alban Institute, 1996). See particularly chapter 6.

10. Seymour, *Aging without Apology*, p. 36.

11. Thibault, *A Deepening Love Affair*, p. 17.

12. Patrick Kavanaugh, *Spiritual Lives of Great Composers* (Grand Rapids, Mich.: Zondervan Publishing House, 1996).

13. Charles Peckham and Arline Peckham, *I Can Still Pray* (Lebanon, Ohio: Otterbein Home, 1979).

14. Susan Coupland, *Beginning to Pray in Old Age: A Parish Life Sourcebook* (Cambridge, Mass.: Cowley Publications, 1985).

15. Ken Dychtwald and Joe Flower, *Age Wave* (Los Angeles: Jeremy P. Tarcher, Inc., 1989). See especially pp. 347-49.

16. Thibault, *A Deepening Love Affair*, p. 83.

17. David Maldonado, "Religion and Persons of Color," in *Aging, Spirituality, and Religion*, Melvin A. Kimble, et al., eds. (Minneapolis: Fortress Press, 1995), p. 119.

18. *Bible Explorations for Adults in Later Life* (Memphis: The Board of Christian Education, Third Age Ministry, 1995), p. 1.

Chapter 5

1. Marlene Wilson, *How to Mobilize Church Volunteers* (Minneapolis: Augsburg Publishing House, 1983), p. 12.

2. Paul Maves, *Older Volunteers in Church and Community* (Valley Forge, Pa.: Judson Press, 1988).

3. Maves, *Older Volunteers*, p. 14.

Chapter 6

1. Lydia Bronte, *The Longevity Factor* (New York: HarperCollins Publishers, 1993).

2. Don Aslett, *Clutter's Last Stand* (Cincinnati: Writer's Digest Books, 1984).

3. Dosia Carlson, *God's Glory II* (Phoenix: Beatitudes Center D.O.A.R., 1997).

4. R. Scott Sullender, *Losses in Later Life: A New Way of Walking with God* (Mahwah, N.J.: Paulist Press, 1989).

5. Sullender, *Losses in Later Life*, p. 79.

6. See United Church of Sun City listed in appendix A.

7. Kathleen Fischer, *Winter Grace: Spirituality for the Later Years* (New York: Paulist Press, 1985), p. 159.

Chapter 7

1. Sarah Louise Delany and Annie Elizabeth Delany with Amy Hill Hearth, *Having Our Say: The Delany Sisters' First 100 Years* (New York: Kodansha International: 1993).

2. Lynn Peters Adler, *Centenarians: The Bonus Years* (Santa Fe, N.M.: Health Press, 1995).

3. Adler, *Centenarians*, p. 150.

4. Joan Lukens, ed., *Affirmative Aging: A Creative Approach to Longer Life* (Harrisburg, Pa.: Morehouse Publishing, 1994), p. 101.

5. 1995 White House Conference on Aging, *The Road to an Aging Policy for the 21st Century*, Final Report, February 1996, p. 302.

6. Harold George Koenig, Mona Smiley, and Jo Ann Ploch Gonzales, *Religion, Health and Aging* (Westport, Conn.: Greenwood Press, 1988).

7. Koenig, Smiley, and Gonzales, *Religion, Health, and Aging*, p. 156.

8. For details contact the Volunteer Interfaith Caregivers Program listed in appendix A.

9. Christine Root, *Health Care for All: A Matter of Faith and Justice* (East Lansing, Mich.: Health and Economic Justice Working

Group, 1993). To obtain a copy see Health and Economic Justice Working Group listed in appendix A.

Chapter 8
1. Julia Cameron and Mark Bryan, *The Artist's Way: A Spiritual Path to Higher Creativity* (New York: G. P. Putnam's Sons, 1992).
2. Erik Erikson, *Childhood and Society* (New York: W. W. Norton, 1963).
3. L. Eugene Thomas and Susan Eisenhandler, *Aging and the Religious Dimension* (Westport, Conn: Auburn House, 1994).
4. Mary Baird Carlsen, *Creative Aging: A Meaning-Making Perspective* (New York: W. W. Norton & Company, Inc., 1991).
5. Philip L. Berman and Connie Goldman, *The Ageless Spirit* (New York: Ballantine Books, 1992), p. 152.
6. Cameron and Bryan, *The Artist's Way*, p. 211.

Chapter 9
1. Erik Erikson, *Childhood and Society*, 2nd ed. rev. (New York: Norton, 1963).
2. Robert Butler, "The Life Review: An Interpretation of Reminiscence in the Aged," *Psychiatry* 26 (1963): 65-76.
3. Harry McMahan and Gloria McMahan. *Grandma Was Quite a Girl* (Escondido, Calif.: McMahan, 1980).
4. Contact Bi-Folkal Productions listed in appendix A.
5. Harry Berman, *Interpreting the Aging Self: Personal Journals in Later Life.* (New York: Springer Publishing Company, Inc., 1994).
6. James E. Birren and Donna E. Deutchman, *Guiding Autobiography Groups for Older Adults* (Baltimore: The Johns Hopkins University Press, 1991).
7. Birren and Deutchman, *Guiding Autobiography Groups*, p. 60.
8. Ann Broyles, *Journaling: A Spirit Journey* (Nashville: Upper Room Books, 1988).
9. Anthony de Mello, S.J. *Wellsprings: A Book of Spiritual Exercises* (New York: Doubleday, 1984).
10. Richard L. Morgan, *Remembering Your Story: A Guide to Spiritual Autobiography* (Nashville: Upper Room Books, 1996).
11. Morgan, *Remembering Your Story*, p. 19.
12. Zalman Schachter-Shalomi and Ronald S. Miller, *From Age-*

ing to Sage-ing: A Profound New Vision of Growing Older (New York: Warner Books, Inc., 1995).

Chapter 10

1. Harriet Kerr Swenson, *Visible and Vital: A Handbook for the Aging Congregation* (New York: Paulist Press, 1994), p. 67.

2. *Understanding Senior Housing for the 1990s* (Washington, D.C.: American Association of Retired Persons, 1990), p. 3.

3. *Understanding Senior Housing for the 1990s*, p. 75.

4. See Church Council of Greater Seattle listed in appendix A.

5. Susan McClelland and Susan McClelland Prescott, *If There's Anything I Can Do for You* (Gainesville, Fla.: Triad Publishing Company, 1990). Duane A. Ewers with Bishop Fritz Mutti, *A Ministry of Caring* (Nashville: Interactive Resources, 1994).

6. Sheelagh McGurn, *Under One Roof* (Park Ridge, Ill.: Parkside Publishing, 1992).

7. Sally A. Reisacher and Roland Hornbostel, *A Home Away from Home: A Consumer Guide to Board and Care Homes and Assisted Living Facilities* (Washington, D.C.: American Association of Retired Persons), p. 23.

8. Henry C. Simmons and Mark A. Peters, *With God's Oldest Friends: Pastoral Visiting in the Nursing Home* (New York: Paulist Press, 1996), p. 93.

9. Simmons and Peters, *With God's Oldest Friends*, p. 101.